Footprints

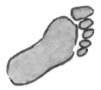

Steps to a Healthy Life
SECOND EDITION

Krishan Hansen
Timothy J. Kahn

Brandon, Vermont

The authors of this workbook would like to specifically acknowledge and thank some of the professionals who have defined and set the standards in this field. A number of the concepts in this book have been borrowed directly from and inspired by these professionals: Gerry Blassingame and the work that he has done as well as the presentations and resources that he has provided; David Hingsburger and all of the resources that he has provided to the DD community; Jim Haaven, whose presentations and pioneering work in this field have provided the concepts of "New Me and Old Me" along with many other concepts and perspectives; Tim Horton continues to provide us with creative ways to work with this population; and work in the field and recent publicatons by Robin Wilson and Michele Burns, as well as Julie Brown have been a great resource to our work.

Note to clinicians: You can download a copy of the Footprints Clinicians Guide *free of charge at the Safer Society Press web site: www.safersociety.org.*

Copyright © 2012 Krishan Hansen and Timothy Kahn
Second Edition

All rights reserved. No part of this publication may be reproduced, stored in a retrieval system, or transmitted in any form or by any means, electronic, mechanical, photocopying, recording, or otherwise without prior written permission of the copyright owners, except for brief quotations included in a review of the book.

Printed in the United States of America
10 9 8 7 6 5 4 3 2 1

ISBN-13 978-1-884444-93-7

P.O. Box 340
Brandon, Vermont 05733 USA
(802) 247-3132
www.safersociety.org

Safer Society Press is a program of the Safer Society Foundation, a 501(c)3 nonprofit dedicated to the prevention and treatment of sexual abuse. For more information visit our web site at www.safersociety.org

Visit our web site, call, or mail a request to order
Footprints: Steps to a Healthy Life, Second Edition
$25 plus shipping and handling
Order #WP156

This is my *Footprints* workbook.

I take good care of it and keep it in a safe place.

My name is:

_____

My age is:

_____

I started this workbook on:

_____

My Progress Chart

STEP 1 Who Am I?	I have: ❏ written my list of rules ❏ written my self letter
STEP 2 What Is Counseling?	I have: ❏ written my list of problems ❏ written my list of goals ❏ created a daily journal or star chart for tracking my progress
STEP 3 Right Touching	I have: ❏ signed my commitment to right touching
STEP 4 My History	I have: ❏ written out my history ❏ written my four wrong steps
STEP 5 Boundaries	I have: ❏ created my boundaries sheet
STEP 6 Sexuality and Relationships	I have: ❏ created my healthy fantasy scrapbook ❏ filled out my CS forms ❏ created my Thought STOP cards
STEP 7 Right Thinking	I have: ❏ created my Thinking Error Cards ❏ written my list of values
STEP 8 Triggers	I have: ❏ written my list of triggers
STEP 9 Danger Zones	I have: ❏ written my list of danger zones and escape plans

STEP 10 Choices		I have: ❑ written my list of triggers and my choices ❑ filled out my S.O.D.A. worksheet to help me consider my choices
STEP 11 Feelings		I have: ❑ used my anger worksheets to control my anger ❑ created my plan for relaxing
STEP 12 Behavior Cycles		I have: ❑ created my offending cycle ❑ created my negative behavior cycle ❑ created my positive behavior cycle
STEP 13 Victims and Empathy		I have: ❑ written my letter to someone who hurt me ❑ written my letter to someone I hurt
STEP 14 My Plan for Staying Safe		I have: ❑ created my plan for staying safe
STEP 15 Putting It All Together		I have: ❑ put my treatment notebook together with everything I have learned
STEP 16 Living the Steps		I have: ❑ written my new self letter ❑ written my Healthy Living for a New Me contract ❑ written my rules
What else are you working on now?		My own goals: ❑ _____ ❑ _____ ❑ _____

Contents

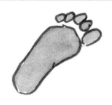

What Is in This Book?   1

Step 1   Who Am I?   5
Step 2   What Is Counseling?   25
Step 3   Right Touching   45
Step 4   My History   63
Step 5   Boundaries   87
Step 6   Sexuality and Relationships   101
Step 7   Right Thinking   133
Step 8   Triggers   149
Step 9   Danger Zones   157
Step 10   Choices   169
Step 11   Feelings   181
Step 12   Behavior Cycles   201
Step 13   Victims and Empathy   219
Step 14   My Plan for Staying Safe   235
Step 15   Putting It All Together   247
Step 16   Living the Steps   261

Words to Know   276

Flash Cards

What Is in This Book?

Welcome to *Footprints*! This book has 16 steps. All of these steps will be important in your life. With the help of your counselor you can decide which steps to take first.

The progress chart at the beginning of this book will help you keep track of the steps you complete so you can see how much you have done. You can also add your own steps and goals to your progress chart like graduating from high school or a work training program, getting a job, or anything else that you are working on. As you make progress, or as your goals change, it is a good idea to go back to the progress chart and add more or make changes. Have fun setting and meeting your own goals!

Footprints is designed to help you take the right steps to being a New Me. This is a good time to define what your New Me is like. At the end of each step (or chapter) in this book there is a chart showing what your New Me can learn from the step. The chart also shows what happens when the Old Me does not use the information from the step. At the bottom of each chart there is a place for you to draw, write, or put pictures of what your New Me rewards and Old Me consequences are. There's an example of this chart on the next page.

Rewards are good things you get when you take steps toward your New Me.

Consequences are what happen when you have Old Me behaviors.

New Me	Old Me
In this space you will see all the things your New Me can learn from a step.	In this space you will see all the things that happen when your Old Me doesn't make good choices.
New Me Rewards In this space you will draw, write, or paste a picture of what your reward is when you make New Me choices.	**Old Me Consequences** In this space you will draw, write, or paste a picture of what your consequence is when you make Old Me choices.

Many people in treatment find it helpful to keep a *Footprints* **scrapbook** or a treatment notebook. This is a book or binder where you can keep handouts and assignments from treatment. It can help to remind you what is important along the way.

At the end of each step you will find this picture with suggestions for what you can put into your scrapbook from the step. Some assignments are specially made to go in your *Footprints* scrapbook. Each one of these special assignments will have this picture on the page before it.

Of course, you should always put your *Footprints* workbook and *Footprints* scrapbook in a safe place where they won't get lost. Some clients like to take their books home so they can look at them on their own. Other clients like to keep them in their counselor's office so they always know where they are. If you take your books home, you will need to make sure you always bring them with you when you go to your counselor's office.

 At the end of each step you will see this picture. This picture marks the self-talk you will learn from the step. **Self-talk** is what you can say out loud or inside your head to keep you on the right path.

Your counselor might want you to do the steps in a different order than they are in this book, and that's okay. They'll still work to help you control your body and keep you on the right path.

There are also **flash cards** that go with your *Footprints* workbook. These cards can help you learn and use the skills from this book. When you see this symbol ⚡ it means there is a flash card to help you use a skill in your life. You can get the flash cards from the back of this book or from your counselor.

These flash cards are intended to help you be a happy, healthy New Me. Some of them may have private information about you. Everyone has a right to privacy. You and your counselor should talk about how to use them privately and what to do if someone asks you about them.

STEP 1
Who Am I?

If you are reading this workbook, it is because somebody wants to help you take steps to control your body and how you act around other people so that you will have a happy and healthy life.

If you work hard in Footprints, you will feel good about yourself. You will have skills to solve problems. People who care about you will be proud of your hard work.

You will notice that at the bottom of each page there are two boxes like this: ☐☐ One box is for you to put your initials in after you finish the page and the other box is for your counselor to initial after reviewing the page with you.

Many people are now getting help controlling their sexual behavior, so you are not alone. There is more good news. By learning the skills in Footprints, you will prepare yourself for a happy and healthy life.

Some of the information in this book is private. "Private" means just for you. You will learn more about this in Step 5 when we learn about boundaries. Before you go further, make sure you know what things are private, who you can talk to about private issues, and who you can share this book with. If you have questions or feel confused, ask your counselor for help.

You probably have other people who care about you and spend time with you. These people are part of your **support team**. Your support team includes your counselor, your family, your teachers or staff members, and your close friends. If you share your work with them, your support team will help you practice the new skills you are learning in *Footprints*.

With your counselor's help, write down the names of people you might share your *Footprints* work with:

1. _____

2. _____

3. _____

Working in *Footprints* may give you strong feelings, like feeling mad or sad or bad, or feeling like you want to have sex. Make sure you and your counselor have a plan for handling these feelings in a good way. In *Footprints* you will learn new behaviors, new ways to do things, and new ways to handle your feelings.

Footprints is hard work, but it will help you be healthy and happy! With your counselor, family, or other support people, try to do a little bit every day. It might take a long time to finish *Footprints*, but that's okay! It takes time to learn new behaviors.

By completing this workbook, you will learn skills to be happy and healthy. You can be proud of your behavior and hard work. You and your counselor, group home staff, friend, parent, or foster parent may also set up rewards for you as you finish assignments and steps in *Footprints*. Make it fun and reward yourself for taking each step.

There are assignments in this book that can be completed in many different ways. You can write, draw pictures, cut out pictures from magazines or use a camera to take pictures, and you can get help from your counselor. You and your counselor can decide how to answer each question. Be creative and have fun!

One of the first steps is learning about who you are. Now, here is your first assignment!

Footprints is meant to help you in all parts of your life, so it is important to learn a little bit about who you are. Please go ahead and write in this book.

Assignment 1A

What is your full name? _____

What is your birth date? _____

Where do you live right now? _____

Who do you live with? _____

What are your favorite foods? _____

Do you have a job right now?   YES   or   NO

If yes, what is it? _____

What do you like to do in your free time?

_____

_____

_____

Who is in your family? List their names and ages:

_____

_____

_____

Do you have any pets right now?   YES   or   NO

If yes, what kind are they, and what are their names?

_____

Who do you spend most of your time with?

_____

Who is on your support team?

_____

_____

(This question is important. Your support team may include your counselor, members of your treatment group, some of the people you live with, support staff, caseworker, family, and friends. Get help if you're not sure. Your support team will be a big part of helping you succeed. People on your support team may need to know some of your private information and keep it private. Learn more in Step 5.)

Who can you talk to about private things?

_____

_____

(This is important because some people get strong sexual feelings when they work in *Footprints*. You and your counselor should make a plan for what to do when these feelings happen.)

Who in the whole world do you respect (look up to) the most right now?

_____

Why? _____

Who is your best friend? _____

Good job, thanks for sharing! This information will help your counselor get to know you better. Now we are going to talk about rules, and why rules keep us safe.

Assignment 1B

 STOP! This part is very important.

 GO. Rules help keep us safe, and they keep us out of jail.

Look at John's list of rules that he uses to keep himself safe:

> John's Rules
>
> 1. I will be honest.
> 2. I will respect boundaries.
> 3. I will make healthy choices.
> 4. I will listen to my support staff.
> 5. I will treat others with respect.
>
> These are my rules using my words. I will add to these rules as I learn more.
>
> —John Smith, 12/26/2012

What are your rules for safe behavior? Some might be treatment rules, house rules, and/or probation rules. You may attach a copy of these rules if they are already written out. On the next page put your rules into words you know. You can write or draw pictures and then go over your list to make sure you know your rules.

After you write your rules on the next page, make a copy of your list to share with your support team and put a copy in your *Footprints* scrapbook.

My Rules

1. _____

   _____

2. _____

   _____

3. _____

   _____

4. _____

   _____

5. _____

   _____

6. _____

   _____

These are my rules using my words. I will add to these rules as I learn more.

_____ , _____
(Sign your name)   (Write the date)

 Assignment 1C

This assignment is a drawing. In the drawing, try to put in as much information from the first assignment (1A) as possible. You may use pictures or words.

Suggestion: Use separate paper for more space! Have fun!

1. Me	2. My Home
3. My Friend	4. My Family

Assignment 1D

Self letter. This next assignment is to help you and your counselor get to know you a little better. You will write a letter to yourself by answering some questions. Your counselor can write down your answers and put them into a letter, you can write it yourself, or you can find pictures that you like.

Here's what Miguel talked about when writing his self letter, his letter to himself:

"Hi, my name is Miguel. I sometimes read my letter when I need help remembering what is important to me."

Here is Miguel's letter:

November 16, 2012

Dear Miguel,

I am 35 and I live in a house with three other men. I feel good. I am really happy because it is going to be my birthday. I like going to work. I am happy to be seeing my mom. I like doing exercise. I like playing football. I like the Seattle Seahawks. I don't like that I sometimes get aroused by children.

I don't like being labeled as a sex offender. I don't like not being able to talk to kids. My main problems are getting aroused by children and not controlling my anger. I want to turn myself around. I want to keep going to therapy. I want to keep following my rules. I plan to stay with my support staff. I want to do well at my job.

I want other people to see that I stay out of trouble. I want people to look to me as a role model. I would like to get back with my girlfriend. I plan to keep living in my program. In order to meet my goals I need to keep staying on track in my support home and use all that I have learned. I need to develop healthy relationships.

Sincerely,
Miguel

16   Step 1: Who Am I?

Edward also did a self letter. He decided to use pictures in his letter. He and his counselor completed the assignment together.

November 26, 2012

Dear Edward,

I am 29-years-old. I like baseball ⚾ and friends and family 👤👤👪.

I am good at working hard 🏋 and being a good friend ☺. It makes me sad ☹ when I think about all the trouble 🚓 that I got in.

My main problem is getting angry 💣. In the future I want to be happy ☺, finish school 🚌, get a job 🔧, and have a girlfriend ♡.

Sincerely,

Edward

Now it is your turn. This assignment may be a little harder and you may need some help. Your counselor can write for you if that helps. On the next three pages, write a letter to yourself and include what you would like to do in the future, how you would like to feel, and what you want others to think of you. You can use words, draw pictures, or cut out pictures from magazines.

This letter is a way of thinking about your goals for treatment as well as goals for your life. You may write down your goals for as far into the future as you would like to go. Remember the letter should contain all three parts: what you want to do, how you want to feel, and how you want others to think of you.

Once you answer the questions, you can put them together into a final copy to share with your support team and put in your scrapbook.

Self Letter

Date _____

Dear _____,
      (You)

1. Who are you (how old are you, where do you live)?

   _____
   _____

2. Describe how you feel about yourself now. Include five positive things that you like about yourself:

   _____
   _____
   _____
   _____
   _____

3. Describe how it feels to have sexual behavior problems or to be labeled as a sex offender:

   _____
   _____
   _____

4. Describe what you think your main problems are:

_____

_____

_____

_____

5. Explain how you would like to feel in the future:

_____

_____

_____

_____

6. What are you good at? Describe personal strengths you would like to build on in the future:

_____

_____

_____

_____

7. Describe how you would like others to view you in the future:

_____

_____

_____

_____

8. Describe what you would like to do in the future (for example, family, relationships, job):

_____

_____

_____

_____

9. Describe what you need to do to accomplish your goals, especially what helps you not get in trouble for wrong touching:

_____

_____

_____

_____

Sincerely, _____
(You)

Good work! Now let's review what we've learned in Step 1 of *Footprints*.

 Assignment 1E

Use pictures or words to fill in the bottom of this chart with your rewards and consequences.

New Me	Old Me
I go the right way when: I use my support team. I follow my rules. I reach my goals. I know what I want and am learning good ways to get it.	I go the wrong way when: Old Me ignores my support team. Old Me ignores my rules. Old Me doesn't do the work.
New Me Rewards	**Old Me Consequences**

Step 1: Who Am I?
Test

Date: _____

1. My counselor is part of my support team.

   　　　　　　　　TRUE　　or　　FALSE

2. The bus driver is part of my support team.

   　　　　　　　　TRUE　　or　　FALSE

3. Who is on your support team?

   _____
   _____
   _____
   _____

4. Who can you talk to about private things?

   _____
   _____

5. My counselor helps me learn to make good choices.

    TRUE   or   FALSE

6. My rules help me stay safe.

    TRUE   or   FALSE

7. It is okay to tell my private information to the grocery clerk.

    TRUE   or   FALSE

6. Being respectful is a good rule.

    TRUE   or   FALSE

7. I like it when people are honest with me.

    TRUE   or   FALSE

8. When I am upset I do not have to follow my rules.

    TRUE   or   FALSE

9. What are three good things about you?

_____

_____

_____

10. Have you initialed each page in Step 1?

    YES   or   NO

24   Step 1: Who Am I?

   "I know my rules."

   Your scrapbook should now include the following items from this step:

  ☐ Your list of rules

  ☐ Your self letter

   There is a flash card to help you remember your rules and what is important to you.

Good job! You have finished the first step! You are moving toward a healthy and happy life.

STEP 2
What Is Counseling?

Counseling is talking with a person who knows how to help you control your body and brain in good ways. A counselor has special training in how to help. Counseling is a good way to stop wrong sexual behavior or wrong touching.

Wrong touching means touching someone else's private parts without permission or touching your own private parts (the places covered by a bathing suit) in public. Wrong touching can also include touching children.

People all over the world use counseling to stop wrong touching. There are many reasons to stop wrong touching.

Wrong touching can make a person feel strong, powerful, or excited. But wrong touching leads to big trouble. Sometimes people doing wrong touching want to stop but they can't, so they get help through counseling.

Let's look at some of the reasons that other people came up with for stopping wrong touching:

- I might get in trouble with my support staff for not following directions.
- It might hurt the other person.
- Other people will pick on me.
- I don't want to go back to jail.
- Other people will tease me.
- People will hate me.
- I won't be able to get a job.
- I will get in trouble with my family.
- I might get in trouble with my treatment group.
- The police might arrest me.

In this list, there are some bad things that might happen if you don't stop wrong touching. Now let's look at some good things that will happen if you do stop wrong touching:

 Good Things that Will Happen When I Don't Do Wrong Touching

1. People will like me.

2. I will feel good when I treat other people nicely.

3. My counselor will give me more responsibility because I am doing well.

4. My family will be proud of me.

5. My support staff will be proud of me.

6. I will not go to jail.

7. People won't think I am weird or strange.

8. I won't get into trouble as much.

9. I won't be afraid of being arrested.

10. I won't have to go to court and talk to a judge.

There are many other reasons to control your sexual behavior. Controlling your sexual behavior means not doing wrong touching. You probably have your own reasons for stopping wrong touching.

Assignment 2A

What are your reasons for controlling your sexual behavior?

1. _____

_____

2. _____

_____

3. _____

_____

Other Problems

Counseling can help you with more than just controlling your sexual behavior. Counseling can help you with other problems as well. Problems that hurt or bother you can keep you from feeling good and getting what you want. Here is a list of other problems that people are working on in counseling:

- I get turned on by kids.
- I don't have any friends.
- I don't like asking people to go out with me.
- I always get into trouble.

- I use drugs and alcohol.
- I have a bad temper.
- I am always fighting.
- I am always bored.
- I never get asked out.
- I need to keep myself clean.

 Assignment 2B

Now it is your turn. What are some problems in your life that you would like to work on? You can choose two problems from the list above but then come up with at least three on your own.

My Problems

1. _____
2. _____
3. _____
4. _____
5. _____
6. _____
7. _____

The next step in working on problems is setting goals. Goals are things that we want to have or want to do. Here are some goals that other people set:

- I will be able to talk about my feelings without fighting.
- I will feel good about who I am.
- I will have friends.
- I will stop hurting people.
- I will control my anger.
- I will get a job.
- I will graduate from school.
- I will never commit a sexual offense again.
- I will live on my own.
- I will take care of myself.
- I will find a girlfriend/boyfriend.
- I will exercise more.
- I will take a shower every day.
- I will keep my room clean.
- I will stop taking things from other people.
- I will stop smoking.
- I will save some money.

 Assignment 2C

Now it is your turn. Make a list of goals that you want to work on. Pick two from the list on the previous page and then make up three of your own.

 Make a copy of this sheet to share with your support team and put in your scrapbook.

My Goals

1. _____
_____

2. _____
_____

3. _____
_____

4. _____
_____

5. _____
_____

You can add these goals to your progress chart. As you reach your goals you can add to this list or make changes.

Telling the Truth

Telling the truth (being honest) is an important part of counseling. Being honest is a New Me behavior. Lying and keeping secrets are Old Me behaviors which may have gotten you in trouble and hurt other people.

Here is how Ted talks about how he stopped his touching problem:

> "Hi, my name is Ted. I had a touching problem and I was touching young children in my neighborhood. I was about 17 years old when I first started doing the wrong touching to kids.
>
> Now I am 33 years old and I haven't done any bad private part touching for three years. Now I live in a house with support staff. I meet with a counselor every week so that I don't touch kids and so I can learn ways to be healthy and happy without getting into trouble. I have support staff that help me follow my rules and have fun.
>
> I also meet with a group once a week to help me make good choices. You should NOT be afraid in group. We try and help each other in group. I tell the truth to the people in my group and to my counselor."

Notice that Ted talked about having a counselor, having a group, and telling the truth. Another way of saying "telling the truth" is "being honest." Being honest is one of the most important ways you can be a New Me and live a healthy life.

Counselors and Groups

Counselors are people who know how to help people in lots of different ways. Counselors can teach people how to control their bodies so that they will not do Old Me behaviors. Counselors care about people and help them succeed in life.

Groups are when three or more people sit down together to help each other make good choices. Groups help people with touching problems feel like they are not alone. Groups help people learn to control their bodies in good ways. Groups help people to stay out of jail. You and your counselor can decide if there is a group that will be helpful to you.

It is sometimes scary to be in a group to talk about private problems. Most people learn to like groups, because in groups they get support and help. Plus, it feels good to know that you are not alone.

Groups work best when everyone agrees to follow rules. If you are in a group, your counselor may have everybody in the group make a list of group rules. Rules make groups safe. Rules make groups a good place to be. Let's look at some rules that you can learn to help your group be a safe place.

Group Rules

1. Arrive on time and leave on time. Show that you care about your group by being ready on time.

2. Sit still in your chair. Sitting in groups is hard, but you can't show you care about others if you are out of your chair.

3. Let one person talk at a time, and look at the person who is talking.

4. Show that you care about other group members. Listen to them and do not talk when they are talking.

5. Ask questions about what the other group member is talking about. This shows that you care.

6. When you hear a group member using right thinking, tell them you are proud of them. When you hear wrong thinking, try to nicely suggest something that would be right thinking. You will learn more about right thinking and wrong thinking later on in *Footprints*.

If you follow these rules, your group will be a great place to be and it will help you stay out of trouble!

 Assignment 2D

Another way that Ted helps himself is by using a daily journal or a star chart to keep track of how he is doing everyday. At the end of the week he shares his chart with his counselor and group.

A **daily journal** is when you write down who you're with and how you feel each day. A **star chart** is where you give yourself a star when you have a good day, when you do certain things you are trying to do, or when you use New Me behaviors.

On the next pages, there are some examples of daily journals and star charts. With your counselor you will choose or create one that works best for you. Your star chart should include some of the goals that you listed in this step.

You will notice that on these two daily journals the bottom of the form has a place for you to fill out how many times you masturbate:

M= _____

and what fantasies you have

Fantasy: _____

Step 6 talks more about why this is important. If you are ready, you and your counselor can jump ahead and learn more about this now or you may decide to wait until later.

📅 Daily Journal 📅

Name: _____

Date: _____ Day of week: _____

Time awake in morning: _____ Time to bed at night: _____

Describe what you did today, including who you were with and how you felt.

_____

_____

_____

_____

_____

_____

_____

Date/Time Completed

Date: _____ Time: _____ M= _____

Fantasy: _____

Fantasy: _____

Daily Journal 📅

Name:_____

Date:_____ Day of week: _____

Time awake in morning: _____ Time to bed at night: _____

Describe what you did today, including who you were with and how you felt.

_____

_____

_____

How mad did you get today?   0   1   2   3   4   5

Why? _____

What did you do?_____

What would you do differently next time: _____

_____

What other feelings did you have? _____

_____

Fantasy: _____ M=_____

Fantasy: _____ M=_____

On the next page is an example of a star chart that Emily uses with her support staff every day or twice a day (at the end of a staff member's shift). It is important for Emily to help fill the form out so that she can help take charge of her life. Star charts work best when they have just a few goals (this one has more to give you more ideas). Pick goals that are important to you.

Make sure that you use your daily journal or your star chart every day. It is important that people in your support team can help you track your progress. You and your counselor can set up rewards to help you remember your charts.

Goal	AM	PM	AM	PM	AM	PM	AM	PM	AM	PM	AM	PM	AM	PM
Follow rules														
Follow meal plan														
Respect others														
Clean clothes														
Clean body														
Avoid children														
Appropriate TV shows														
Exercise														
Do chores														
Stay active during the day														
Staff initials and my initials														

Star Chart

Assignment 2E

Fill in your rewards and consequences on the chart below.

New Me	Old Me
I avoid my problems and work on my goals. I keep track of my progress. I use counseling to help me get the good things that I want.	The Old Me doesn't work on my goals. The Old Me doesn't learn to control my behaviors. The Old Me doesn't let people help me. The Old Me keeps making the same mistakes.
New Me Rewards	**Old Me Consequences**

Step 2: What Is Counseling?
Test

Date: _____

1. The New Me can use counseling to work toward my goals.

    TRUE   or   FALSE

2. Lots of people get help using counseling.

    TRUE   or   FALSE

3. Why are you in counseling?

   _____

   _____

4. The Old Me had problems with doing wrong touching to other people.

    TRUE   or   FALSE

5. I will get in trouble if I talk about things in counseling.

    TRUE   or   FALSE

6. I sometimes have problems controlling my anger.

    TRUE   or   FALSE

7. I have problems with the following: (Circle all that apply.)

    A. Touching

    B. Yelling

    C. Fighting

    D. Stealing

    E. Lying

    F. Respecting boundaries

8. I have the following goals: (Circle all that apply.)

    A. I will be nice to people.

    B. I will control my anger.

    C. I will talk nicely.

    D. I will stop stealing.

    E. I will tell the truth.

    F. I will respect boundaries.

9. What do you use to keep track of your progress? (Circle all that apply.)

    Daily Journals   Star Charts

10. What goals can you work on this week?

_____

_____

"I will use counseling to help me get to my goals."

Your scrapbook should now include the following items from this step:

☐ Your list of problems

☐ Your list of goals

☐ Your daily journal or star chart

There is a flash card to help you remember your goals.

Congratulations! You have completed Step 2.

STEP 3
Right Touching

Footprints is a book that helps people control their sexual behavior and stop wrong touching. Wrong touching is sometimes called **a touching problem**. Anybody can have a touching problem. Touching problems are when a person touches another person in a bad way, especially when the person's private parts are touched. **Private parts** are a person's bottom, chest, penis, or vagina. If you don't know these words, talk to your counselor.

Boundaries

When things are private that means just for you. We put up boundaries around things that are private. The walls and the door on your bedroom are boundaries. The bathroom door is a boundary. The clothes on your body are a boundary. When the bathroom door is closed, that means do not come in.

There are also invisible boundaries, like your body boundary. One way to know your body boundary is to put your arm out in front of you. That is your space. Some people call this their bubble, and they don't like people getting too close to them, or getting inside their bubble. There are also invisible boundaries around the things you own, things you don't want other people to touch. Think of it this way, there are boundaries around things that are private or just for you.

Knowing what is private and knowing boundaries are very important. You will learn more about this in Step 5. You and your counselor can practice making sure you know about boundaries. Group is a also good place to learn more about boundaries. Group and counseling are places that you can talk about private things.

Sexual Behavior

People sometimes touch each other's private parts in healthy ways. This kind of touching is called **sexual touching**, or **sex**. Some sexual touching is how people make babies. Without sexual touching, babies wouldn't be born. Without good sexual touching people wouldn't have that special good feeling in their bodies. So, sexual touching can be a very good thing.

Good sex. That's right, these two words can go together, but there are some things that you need to learn first. In this step

we will first learn about sexual behavior problems or wrong touching.

Wrong touching and **sexual behavior problems** are behaviors that can lead to trouble and maybe even jail. Sexual behavior is a bad thing when it involves children, or when it hurts or bothers other people, or when it involves force, threats, tricks, lies, or bribes.

Wrong Touching

Wrong touching can include touching children's private parts, touching your own private parts in public places, spying on other people when they are undressing, or talking too much about body parts or private things.

In this book, we also call other sexual behavior problems wrong touching, such as stealing underwear, exposing your private parts, or rubbing up against other people without asking. Sometimes people touch animals in their private parts or hurt animals for fun, which is also wrong touching. There are lots of different kinds of sexual behavior problems and they all lead to trouble.

Some kinds of sexual touching are against the law, and sometimes people who do wrong sexual touching can go to jail. *Footprints* is a book to help people learn to control their bodies so that they will not hurt anyone or go to jail.

Rules for Touching

Here are some rules that you can follow to make sure you never do wrong touching:

1. Never touch anybody without getting permission first.

2. Never do sexual touching with children.

3. Do not touch your own private parts unless you are in a private place, like your bedroom or the bathroom with the door closed.

4. Don't talk to children about sex or sexual body parts.

5. Don't do anything that hurts another person.

6. Make sure you have permission *and* consent before doing touching with your boyfriend or girlfriend.

Permission and Consent

Permission and consent are two very important words. Your treatment rules from Step 1 may have rules about sex. You may need to get permission from your counselor or group before getting into a sexual relationship. **Permission** means that your counselor or support staff says it's okay.

Consent is when your partner agrees to do something. In order to agree to sexual touching:

1. Your partner must be close to your age.

2. Your partner must be able to really understand what is going to happen.

3. Your partner must have the right to say no.

4. Your partner must say yes.

 Assignment 3A

What is the difference between right touching and wrong touching? Use words or draw a picture of right and wrong touching. Include a description of the things that make them different.

Right Touching	**Wrong Touching**

What makes them different?

_____

_____

Assignment 3B

Talking about wrong touching can be hard. Now is a good time to take a break. Draw a picture of your life when you were little. Your counselor will help you label everything in the picture.

Kinds of Touching

Now it is time to learn more about right touching and wrong touching. This next part of *Footprints* is to help you decide what is right touching and what is wrong touching.

Right Touching

Right touching must have consent. **Right touching** is when you ask before you touch and the other person says yes. Right touching is when you touch someone in a nice and caring way.

Right touching can only happen with someone who is your age. For right touching you must know about how to protect yourself and your partner from sexually transmitted diseases and how to protect yourself or your partner from getting pregnant. Right touching is legal, and you do not get in trouble for it.

 When something is **legal**, it is okay to do, and you will not go to jail if you do it.

 When something is **illegal**, it is not okay, and you can get in big trouble if you do it.

Your counselor will have some rules for you about what touching is okay and what touching is not okay. In most cases it is important to talk to your counselor before you do *any* sexual touching.

Step 3: Right Touching

 Assignment 3C

Circle the things that must happen for true consent:

My partner has long hair.

My partner smiles at me.

My partner is the same age.

I use bribes when my partner says no.

My partner says yes.

I use threats to show I'm strong.

We both know what is going on.

I use tricks to get my partner to touch me.

It is okay to say no.

My partner has blue eyes.

My partner winks at me.

I care about my partner.

My partner wears a small shirt.

My partner has brown hair.

My partner hits me.

Wrong Touching

If you touch somebody else in their private parts without their permission, that is wrong touching. If somebody else touches you in your private parts without your permission, that is also wrong touching. If you touch someone's private parts, and they are not old enough or smart enough to understand what it means to do touching with you, that is wrong touching.

Wrong touching is when you touch someone in a mean or hurtful way. It is wrong touching if you use threats, tricks, bribes, or force to get someone to do touching with you.

> A **threat** is when you say you will hurt the other person or lie about them to get them in trouble.
>
> A **trick** is when you say you will do one thing and instead you do sexual touching.
>
> A **bribe** is when you promise to give the other person money or candy or something else they want if they will do sexual touching with you.
>
> **Force** is when you make someone do something.

Wrong touching is illegal, and you can go to jail. Wrong touching is also when you touch somebody in their private parts, and they are in your family. Family private part touching is also called **incest**, and it is wrong touching. Someone in your family could give their consent for touching their private parts, and it would still be wrong touching.

In this book, wrong touching can also include things like stealing underwear, or exposing your private parts, or sexual harassment. **Sexual harassment** is talking about sex or private information when it bothers other people.

 Assignment 3D

Now let's see how this works in real life. For each example below, decide whether it is right touching or wrong touching. Circle the best answer and tell your counselor why you chose that answer.

1. My mom gives me a hug when I see her.

    RIGHT TOUCHING   or   WRONG TOUCHING

2. I run up to people when I see them and surprise them by grabbing them.

    RIGHT TOUCHING   or   WRONG TOUCHING

3. I touch my sister's private parts with a private part of mine.

    RIGHT TOUCHING   or   WRONG TOUCHING

4. I shake hands with my counselor when I see him.

    RIGHT TOUCHING   or   WRONG TOUCHING

5. I hit people so they will know I am strong and tough.

    RIGHT TOUCHING   or   WRONG TOUCHING

6. My support staff gives me a high five.

   RIGHT TOUCHING   or   WRONG TOUCHING

7. My older sister made me put my penis (private part) in her vagina (private part).

   RIGHT TOUCHING   or   WRONG TOUCHING

8. Sometimes I touch my private parts when I am around other people in public.

   RIGHT TOUCHING   or   WRONG TOUCHING

9. Sometimes I touch my private parts when I am alone in my room and the door is closed.

   RIGHT TOUCHING   or   WRONG TOUCHING

10. Sometimes I kiss my boyfriend or girlfriend after asking if it is okay and they say yes.

    RIGHT TOUCHING   or   WRONG TOUCHING

11. Sometimes I rub my private parts in front of other people to show that I like them.

    RIGHT TOUCHING   or   WRONG TOUCHING

Great job! Your counselor will make sure that you understand each of these 11 situations.

56 Step 3: Right Touching

 Assignment 3E

Right touching. Now it is your turn to tell about yourself. Almost everybody does some right touching and some wrong touching. Think about your life. Write down five examples of right touching that you have done in your life:

1. _____

2. _____

3. _____

4. _____

5. _____

 Assignment 3F

Wrong touching. Now write down five examples of wrong touching that you have done in your life:

1. _____

2. _____

3. _____

4. _____

5. _____

 Assignment 3G

Now it is time to make a commitment to control your body and only do right touching. A **commitment** is a very strong promise.

 Make a copy of this page, or make your own, to share with your support team and to put in your scrapbook.

My Commitment to Right Touching

I, _____, will control my body and only do right touching.

I will have permission and consent before I do any touching.

I can control my body.

Signed, _____
(You)

Assignment 3H

Fill in your rewards and consequences below on the chart.

New Me	Old Me
I ask before I touch people. I only do right touching. I know what consent is and how to ask for it. I follow my rules for right touching.	The Old Me goes the wrong way when I forget to ask before touching. The Old Me gets in trouble when I do wrong touching. The Old Me goes the wrong way when I don't think about others.
New Me Rewards	**Old Me Consequences**

Step 3: Right Touching
Test

Date: _____

1. If you wanted to do touching with your partner, what would you do first?

   _____

   _____

2. It is okay to hold hands with your girlfriend or boyfriend when you go to the mall.

           TRUE   or   FALSE

3. It is okay to do sexual touching with someone when there is consent.

           TRUE   or   FALSE

4. My partner should be ___-years-old or older. (Circle the best answer.)

       12   16   18   21   25   35   45

5. If a 14-year-old girl asks me to touch her, it is okay to touch her.

           TRUE   or   FALSE

6. If someone touches me in a bad way, it is best to stay quiet.

           TRUE   or   FALSE

7. Becky likes to sneak up on her older brother and hit him on the bottom when he is not looking. That is:

      RIGHT TOUCHING   or   WRONG TOUCHING

8. Henry asks his girlfriend if he can hold her hand while they watch a movie. She is his age and they both like each other. This is:

      RIGHT TOUCHING   or   WRONG TOUCHING

"I will control my body and only do right touching."

Your scrapbook should now include the following item from this step:

☐ Your commitment to right touching

There is a flash card to help you remember to only do right touching.

Good work. You are now done with Step 3. Reward yourself for a good job. This was a hard step, and you must have done a good job or you wouldn't be reading this right now.

STEP 4
My History

This may be a very hard step. In this step you are going to talk about your history or your past. **History** means things that have already happened. For example, what you did yesterday, what you did last week, and what you did last year is all part of your history.

Some of your history might be sad or embarrassing, but talking about it is a big step toward being happy and healthy. In *Footprints*, one of the things you are learning is to control your sexual behaviors. To do this, it is important to find out where you learned about sexual touching. Once you figure out where you learned about sexual touching, you can then start taking steps to stop wrong touching.

✏️ Assignment 4A

Write down the earliest thing you can remember about your life. This means that you should try to think about when you were very young. Describe what you remember:

_____

_____

_____

_____

How old were you then? _____

✏️ Assignment 4B

Now think about where you first learned about sexual touching. Think about your past. Answer the following questions. If you don't think anybody ever did wrong touching to you, just put "none" in the blanks.

1. How did you first learn about sex?

   _____

   _____

   _____

2. What did you learn?

   _____

   _____

   _____

   _____

   _____

3. Have you ever seen pictures of naked people or pictures of people having sex?

   _____

4. Have you ever been around other people who were doing sexual things?

   _____

5. Who was the first person who ever touched you in a sexual way?

   _____

6. How old were you when it happened? _____ years old

   How old was the other person? _____ years old

7. What did that person do?

   _____

   _____

   _____

Step 4: My History

8. Where were you living when it happened?

   _____

9. How did you feel when the other person did the sexual behavior to you?

   _____

   _____

   _____

10. Who was the second person who ever touched you in a sexual way?

    _____

11. How old were you when it happened? _____ years old

    How old was the other person? _____ years old

12. What did that person do?

    _____

    _____

    _____

13. Where were you living when it happened?

    _____

14. How did you feel when the other person did the sexual behavior to you?

_____

_____

_____

15. Now list all of the other people who have ever touched your private parts or asked you to touch their private parts. Your counselor may have more information about your history that you can add to this list.

_____

_____

_____

_____

Feelings about Sexual Touching

In order to help you stop your sexual touching problems, it is sometimes a good idea to start talking about your feelings instead of keeping them inside. If someone did wrong touching to you, you might have some feelings inside that you don't tell other people about. Sometimes people who have been touched in wrong ways have lots of different feelings. Here is a list of some of them:

- Scared
- Confused
- Angry
- Sexy
- Lonely
- Bored
- Empty
- Ashamed
- Guilty
- Hurt
- Helpless

This is a good time to talk to your counselor about some of your feelings. You will learn more about feelings in Step 11. You can skip ahead to that step now if you are having strong feelings.

Sometimes it also helps to draw a picture about what happened to you. Sometimes pictures work better than words.

Assignment 4C

Draw a picture about someone touching you in a way you didn't like. Ask your counselor to help label each person in the picture. If you want, you can draw on a different piece of paper, and cut out the picture and paste it or staple it on this page.

Touching Other People

Now it is time to talk about sexual touching that you have done to other people. This may be a hard thing to do, but it is very important. Talking about wrong touching can be scary, embarrassing, or just plain hard.

In *Footprints*, you don't have to worry about people thinking bad things about you, or getting into trouble. In *Footprints* we know that it takes a strong and brave person to talk about touching problems.

This is an important time to talk to your counselor about **confidentiality** (what is private) and **mandatory reporting** (what information counselors have to report to police).

Some people have a hard time admitting to mistakes they make. Sometimes they even lie and make up stories to stay out of trouble or to get attention. In *Footprints* it is important to tell the truth and admit to past mistakes so that you can learn to stay out of trouble.

This step will work best if you are completely honest about your history. In *Footprints* you have to tell about your past wrong touching so that you can make a plan to keep from doing it again in the future.

Assignment 4D

Write down five reasons you should tell the truth about your wrong touching. If you can't come up with five reasons, ask for help.

1. _____

2. _____

3. _____

4. _____

5. _____

 Assignment 4E

Now write down five reasons you might not want to tell the whole truth about your wrong touching:

1. _____

2. _____

3. _____

4. _____

5. _____

Even though there are reasons not to be honest, not telling the whole truth about your wrong touching is an Old Me behavior. Not being honest keeps you making Old Me choices. Your counselor can talk to you about more reasons to tell the truth if you need some help. If you are ready to take the next step, it is time to start being honest so you can start making New Me choices.

 Assignment 4F

Remember and write down the first names of everyone you have ever done wrong sexual touching with on the middle line below. If you don't know the person's name, you can use other words like "woman on street" or "boy."

1. _____   _____   _____

2. _____   _____   _____

3. _____   _____   _____

4. _____   _____   _____

5. _____   _____   _____

6. _____   _____   _____

7. _____   _____   _____

8. _____   _____   _____

Assignment 4G

Now go back to your list and write down how old you were when the wrong touching happened with each person on the list. Write down your age on the right side of the person's name. Here's an example:

1. _____   _____Jimmy_____   __18__

 Assignment 4H

Now go back to your list again and write down the age of the other person on the left hand side of the person's name. Here's how the example looks now:

1. __10__   _____Jimmy_____   __18__

So in this example, the first person's name was Jimmy, and he was 10 when the wrong touching happened. The person who did wrong touching was 18 at the time.

Assignment 4I

Write down each person's name again then circle where you touched that person and with what parts of your body you touched them.

1. Name: _____
   Which parts of this person did you touch?
   PENIS   VAGINA   BOTTOM   BREASTS OTHER: _____

   With which parts of your body did you touch them?
   PENIS   VAGINA   BOTTOM   BREASTS OTHER: _____

2. Name: _____
   Which parts of this person did you touch?
   PENIS   VAGINA   BOTTOM   BREASTS OTHER: _____

   With which parts of your body did you touch them?
   PENIS   VAGINA   BOTTOM   BREASTS OTHER: _____

3. Name: _____
   Which parts of this person did you touch?
   PENIS   VAGINA   BOTTOM   BREASTS OTHER: _____

   With which parts of your body did you touch them?
   PENIS   VAGINA   BOTTOM   BREASTS OTHER: _____

4. Name: _____
   Which parts of this person did you touch?
   PENIS   VAGINA   BOTTOM   BREASTS OTHER: _____

   With which parts of your body did you touch them?
   PENIS   VAGINA   BOTTOM   BREASTS OTHER: _____

5. Name: _____

   Which parts of this person did you touch?
   PENIS   VAGINA   BOTTOM   BREASTS   OTHER: _____

   With which parts of your body did you touch them?
   PENIS   VAGINA   BOTTOM   BREASTS   OTHER: _____

6. Name: _____

   Which parts of this person did you touch?
   PENIS   VAGINA   BOTTOM   BREASTS   OTHER: _____

   With which parts of your body did you touch them?
   PENIS   VAGINA   BOTTOM   BREASTS   OTHER: _____

7. Name: _____

   Which parts of this person did you touch?
   PENIS   VAGINA   BOTTOM   BREASTS   OTHER: _____

   With which parts of your body did you touch them?
   PENIS   VAGINA   BOTTOM   BREASTS   OTHER: _____

8. Name: _____

   Which parts of this person did you touch?
   PENIS   VAGINA   BOTTOM   BREASTS   OTHER: _____

   With which parts of your body did you touch them?
   PENIS   VAGINA   BOTTOM   BREASTS   OTHER: _____

Sexual History

Now that you have answered these questions, your counselor will help you complete your **sexual history**. This means putting together all the information you have given into one big picture.

Your sexual history should include all of the following:

- Where you learned about sexual touching or sex
- Touching that other people have done to you
- Touching that you have done to other people
- Any pornography you have seen
- When you started masturbating

Your counselor may ask you other questions, too.

Once you have completed your sexual history you will put it in your scrapbook to look at sometimes and remember all the work you have done to get on the right path.

Taking Wrong Steps

Another way to look at your sexual history is to look at the Old Me steps that you took every time you did wrong touching. When you got in trouble for doing something bad you might feel like things just happened and it was out of your control. Remember that you are in control of your body and the things that you do.

For example, your wrong sexual touching didn't just happen. You took some Old Me steps and did some Old Me thinking to make it happen. In this assignment you will learn about the Old Me steps you made and how to make New Me choices next time.

When you did wrong touching, four things happened first:

1. You got a bad idea.
2. You used wrong thinking.
3. You did some planning.
4. You didn't think about others.

 Assignment 4J

My four wrong steps. Here is an assignment to help you understand the four wrong steps that you took when you got in trouble for wrong touching. (Lisa put her example on the top line to give you some help.)

I GOT A BAD IDEA

I want to . . .

Lisa's example for you: I got the idea to touch my brother.

_____

_____

_____

_____

_____

I USED WRONG THINKING TO DECIDE TO DO IT.

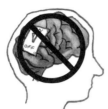

. . . wrong thinking . . .

Lisa's example for you: I told myself I wouldn't get caught. It was no big deal and he wanted to do it.

___

___

___

___

___

My Planning

How did I make this happen . . .

Lisa's example for you: I gave my brother candy.

_____

_____

_____

_____

_____

Ignore Others' Feelings

How did other people try to stop me?

How did I ignore their feelings?

Lisa's example for you: My brother was only three. He cried, but I just thought about what I wanted.

_____

_____

_____

_____

_____

Whenever we do something, there are consequences. **Consequences** are what happens because we did something. There can be good consequences and bad ones. When someone does wrong touching, there are bad consequences. What were the consequences when you did wrong sexual touching?

CONSEQUENCES

 What were the consequences . . .

Lisa's example for you: He got hurt and I got put in jail.

_____

_____

_____

_____

Footprints will help you have good ideas, use right thinking, use good planning, and think about other people. Building up these four skills will help keep you out of trouble and keep you safe.

 Assignment 4K

Put in your rewards and consequences in the chart below.

New Me	Old Me
I am responsible for my behavior. I can talk to the right people about things that I have done. I can learn from my mistakes.	The Old Me blames other people. The Old Me doesn't talk about my feelings. The Old Me ignores the past.
New Me Rewards	**Old Me Consequences**

Step 4: History
Test

Date: _____

1. When is it okay to talk about the wrong touching that you have gotten in trouble for?

   _____

   _____

2. It is okay to talk to the bus driver about my sexual history.

   TRUE   or   FALSE

3. It is okay to tell a new friend about my sexual history.

   TRUE   or   FALSE

4. My sexual history is public information.

   TRUE   or   FALSE

5. Who gets to know your private information?

   _____

   _____

6. Talking about my past can help me learn ways to stay out of trouble.

TRUE   or   FALSE

7. Telling the truth shows people I am serious about staying out of trouble.

TRUE   or   FALSE

8. It is okay to tell stories when I don't feel like talking about something.

TRUE   or   FALSE

9. I am not the only person who has made bad choices in the past.

TRUE   or   FALSE

"I can talk to my counselor or my group about what I did so that I won't do it again."

Your scrapbook should now include the following items from this step:

☐ Your sexual history

☐ Your four wrong steps

There is a flash card to help you to remember to be honest.

Nice work! Understanding your four wrong steps is important. It will help you build up skills and choices that lead to a healthy life.

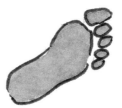

STEP 5
Boundaries

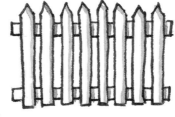

One of the first steps of treatment is learning boundaries. Everyone has boundaries. Boundaries are what separate you and your things from other people and their things. Boundaries help everyone feel safe and protected. Boundaries define what is private and what is public. If something is **private**, it is just for you or just for the other person. If something is **public**, it is meant for everybody.

Boundaries separate your body, your room, and your things from other people. There are also boundaries about what you can say or do and what you should not say or do. Some things are private and some things are public.

Respecting boundaries means that you care about other people, you don't get into other people's things, and you keep your own private things private. If you aren't sure of your boundaries or someone else's boundaries make sure you ask and get permission before you act. Everybody has boundaries. It is important to know what these boundaries are so that you can respect them.

✏️ Assignment 5A

Counselor. Find out what your counselor's boundaries are.

What can you touch (public)? _____
_____

What should you not touch in his or her office (private)? _____
_____

What do you do in the office? _____
_____

✏️ Assignment 5B

Home. There are boundaries everywhere. What are the boundaries at your home? Check with your support staff or housemate to make sure you know the important ones.

What can you touch (public)? _____
_____

What should you not touch (private)? _____

_____

What are the private places in your home? _____

_____

What can you do in the house without asking? _____

_____

✏️ Assignment 5C

Work. What are the boundaries at work? (Check with your job coach to make sure you get the important ones.)

What can you touch (public)? _____

_____

What should you not touch (private)? _____

_____

Who can you talk to? _____

_____

What can you do at work? _____

_____

Assignment 5D

Another support person. Pick one other person on your support team and find out what her or his boundaries are.

Name: _____

What are her or his private things that are off limits? _____

_____

_____

My Personal Boundaries

Now it is time to talk about your personal boundaries. Your boundaries can include:

- Your space
- Your private information
- Your body
- Your bedroom
- Your things
- Your bathroom
- Your bed

These are the things that other people should ask your permission before they touch. A boundary means "stay out unless I say okay."

Your body is private. When things are private that means just for you. Things that are private should happen in private places. Here are some private things:

- Talking about sex
- Thinking someone is sexy
- Changing your clothes
- Scratching or touching your private parts, even through your clothing
- Being naked
- Picking your nose
- Going to the bathroom
- Anything to do with your private parts

Your bedroom is also private. There is a boundary that makes it private: the door. People should ask permission before coming into your room, and you should ask permission before going into their rooms.

Here's how Michael talks about his boundaries:

> "Hi! With my counselor I have written down all of my boundaries. I keep this list in my room so that I can feel safe and the people around me are safe."

Assignment 5E

 Make a copy of the sheet on the next page (or create your own) to share with your support team and to put in your scrapbook.

My Boundaries

This is a list of my private things. These things are just for me:

1. _____

2. _____

3. _____

4. _____

5. _____

Here are some private places that are just for me:

1. _____

2. _____

Other people also have private things that are just for them and not for me. If something is not mine, I ask before touching it or talking about it and wait to see if the person says yes.

Michael also uses a boundaries sheet to show that he knows the boundaries. Here is what Michael has to say:

> "My support staff and I fill out this sheet when I forget my boundaries or when someone around me isn't respecting boundaries. I use this sheet to show my team that I know my boundaries and the boundaries around me."

You and your counselor can change this sheet to make it work for you.

 Assignment 5F

Your counselor will make copies of the next page for you. Fill one out every day for the next week.

Others' Boundaries

1. Describe some situations today where you respected someone else's boundaries:

_____

_____

_____

2. Describe some situations today where you could have done a better job of respecting the boundaries of others:

_____

_____

_____

3. Describe how someone else did not respect boundaries today:

_____

_____

_____

Assignment 5G

Here is a test to see how well you know the difference between private and public. Circle the best answer.

1. My bedroom is: PRIVATE or PUBLIC
2. My body is: PRIVATE or PUBLIC
3. The grocery store is: PRIVATE or PUBLIC
4. The bus is: PRIVATE or PUBLIC
5. Talking about dating is: PRIVATE or PUBLIC

Good job! Your counselor can give you more examples.

When you got in trouble for wrong touching you were not respecting other people's boundaries. Not respecting boundaries is an Old Me behavior. Respecting boundaries now is a good way to show that you will not do wrong touching again. Respecting boundaries is a New Me behavior.

Assignment 5H

Put your rewards and consequences at the bottom of this chart.

New Me	Old Me
I respect boundaries. I know what my boundaries are. I know what other people's boundaries are. I know what is private.	The Old Me forgets to respect boundaries. The Old Me doesn't respect other people's boundaries. The Old Me doesn't respect what is private or not for me.
New Me Rewards	**Old Me Consequences**

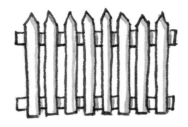

Step 5: Boundaries
Test

Date: _____

1. People get in trouble when they don't respect boundaries.

     TRUE   or   FALSE

2. The door on my bedroom is a boundary.

     TRUE   or   FALSE

3. I respect boundaries when I call people names to tease them.

     TRUE   or   FALSE

4. What boundary did you respect today?

   _____

   _____

5. Even when people don't respect my boundaries I can still respect their boundaries.

     TRUE   or   FALSE

6. An arm's length is a good amount of space to keep in between my body and another person's body.

TRUE   or   FALSE

7. When people don't respect my boundaries, I can do the following: (Circle the best answers.)

    A. Yell

    B. Ignore it

    C. Hit them

    D. Ask them to stop

8. What if that doesn't work? What will you do?

    _____

    _____

9. What should other people do if they see you that you are not respecting boundaries?

    _____

    _____

"I will respect boundaries."

Your scrapbook should now include the following item from this step:

☐ Your boundaries sheet

There is a flash card to remind you to respect boundaries.

Good job! You are moving right along.

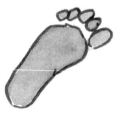

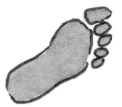

STEP 6
Sexuality and Relationships

This step focuses on sexual feelings and how to control and express them in healthy ways. First, what are sexual feelings and where do they come from?

When you grew from a child into an adult your body went through many changes. These changes were called **puberty**. During puberty your body changed in many ways. You grew hair under your arms and on your private area. If you're a man, your voice might have also changed into a deeper voice. If you're a woman, your breasts might have developed. Also, your body might have started having strong **sexual feelings**.

Sexual feelings are normal. Everybody has sexual feelings. It is part of being human. These are the feelings that you get inside your body when you think about sex. Sometimes sexual feelings are called **urges** or **fantasies**.

Step 6: Sexuality and Relationships

In *Footprints* it is important to not be afraid or ashamed of your sexual feelings. It is important to talk with your counselor about your sexual feelings. There also may be other people in your support team that you can talk to about these feelings. Make sure you know who you can and can't talk to about sexual feelings.

Sexual feelings don't take a timeout while you are in treatment, so this is a step that you will keep coming back to as you work through this book and even after you finish this book. Sometimes it is even a good idea to start with this step. There is a lot of information in this step and you might not be ready for some parts until later. You and your counselor can decide what you are ready to do now.

You are in control of your body and you decide how to control your body when you have feelings, especially sexual feelings. This step will give you some tools for managing your sexual feelings and controlling your body in good ways.

Remember, everybody gets sexual feelings. Sexual feelings are not bad. They are perfectly normal. It is your job to learn how to control your sexual feelings so that you don't hurt other people and so that you don't get into trouble.

Step 6 will help you in four ways:

1. Have healthy sexual fantasies (thoughts about right touching)

2. Decrease unhealthy sexual fantasies (thoughts about wrong touching)

3. Express sexual feelings in healthy ways

4. Build healthy relationships

All four parts need to happen at the same time, but you will learn about them in order first.

 Assignment 6A

Make a list of what words you use when you are feeling sexual. Make sure that you can talk to your counselor about this.

1. _____

2. _____

3. _____

 Assignment 6B

List all of the people that you can talk to about your sexual feelings and urges.

1. _____

2. _____

3. _____

1. Have Healthy Sexual Fantasies (Thoughts)

Masturbation

Masturbation is when you touch your private parts to feel good. Masturbation is a normal healthy behavior when it is done in a private place. Masturbation is an important part of healthy sexuality. It isn't something to be embarrassed about.

Masturbation can lead you to trouble if you are doing it so much that you can't take care of the other things that you need to do. It can lead to trouble if it hurts your body (causing sores or bleeding). It can lead to trouble if you are not in a private place, if it is not a good time, or if you are thinking about doing wrong touching while you are masturbating.

As you will learn later in this step, talking to your counselor and group about sexual feelings and behaviors is an important part of treatment. You might feel embarrassed, but it's good to talk to your counselor about your sexual feelings anyway. This is one of the things your counselor is trained to help you understand. You and your counselor should talk about appropriate masturbation and how to make it a healthy part of your life. Remember, only masturbate when you are thinking about a person who can give consent.

This step will help you have healthy sexual feelings and fantasies. A **sexual fantasy** is something that you think about that gives you strong sexual feelings. For men, sexual fantasies might make their penis get hard (this is called an **erection**). Sexual fantasies are what people think about when they masturbate.

What is a healthy fantasy? A healthy sexual fantasy is when you think about right touching that you won't get in trouble for and that doesn't hurt other people. A healthy fantasy must include consent. You learned a little about consent in Step 3. **Consent** means:

- Your partner is your age.

- Your partner says yes.

- Your partner can say no.

- Your partner is as smart as you are.

- You and your partner know what each other's boundaries are.

- You and your partner know how to avoid getting pregnant and know how to avoid getting sexually transmitted diseases.

- Neither you nor your partner is drunk or taking drugs to get high.

Your counselor may have some questions to ask you and your partner to make sure that you both can give consent. You will learn more about consent later in this step.

One way to increase your healthy sexual fantasies is with a healthy fantasy scrapbook. This is a scrapbook that you create with the help of your counselor. Your scrapbook can include:

- Pictures of men or women your age from magazines
- Romantic stories written on paper or recorded on a tape
- Your own healthy sexual fantasy that you have written or recorded

Rules for Your Scrapbook

1. Keep it in a private place.
2. Review it with your counselor to make sure it is appropriate.
3. Don't show your scrapbook to others, it is private.
4. Don't have pornography in your scrapbook, especially if pornography is one of your triggers. Talk to your counselor about what pornography is if you are not sure.

 Assignment 6C

Create your own healthy fantasy scrapbook. Check it out with your counselor. You may come up with other rules for your scrapbook besides the ones above. Keep it in a safe private place.

 Assignment 6D

There are many things that people can do to help themselves control their sexual urges and to stop feelings about wrong touching. Here is a list of ideas:

- Quickly get away from any children.
- Go tell a support staff person.
- Masturbate in private to a good fantasy (right touching).
- Do something fun to get your mind off it.
- Tell your brain to stop, and think about what might happen in the future if you do wrong touching (consequences).
- Get some serious physical exercise to wear yourself out.
- Do 30 jumping jacks in your bedroom.
- Think about how awful it would be to go to jail.
- Think about how other people would feel disappointed in you.
- Yell NO inside your head, and do something else.
- Have positive or healthy sexual fantasies.

List three things that work for you to help control your sexual feelings and only think about right touching:

1. _____
2. _____
3. _____

2. Decrease Unhealthy Sexual Fantasies (Thoughts about Wrong Touching)

Along with having healthy fantasies, this step will help you decrease your unhealthy fantasies, also called deviant fantasies. **Unhealthy fantasies** are the thoughts, feelings, urges, and impulses that some people have about wrong touching. Unhealthy fantasies often lead to offending, wrong touching, and trouble.

One way for a man to find out if he is having unhealthy fantasies is with a plethysmograph. A plethysmograph is a way of looking at what thoughts and fantasies make your penis get hard. This is called **arousal**. During a plethysmograph, a rubber band attached to a machine measures your penis while you listen to or look at tapes or pictures of different sexual activities.

Plethysmographs don't work for everyone. You and your counselor can decide if you should have a plethysmograph. There are other ways to examine your fantasies. Measuring your arousal to right touch and wrong touch fantasies is one way to show that you are making progress.

This step will help you reduce your unhealthy fantasies. When you got the idea of wrong touching that was a unhealthy fantasy. There are two main ways to decrease unhealthy fantasies:

1. Controlling impulses
2. Controlling your arousal

Impulses or **urges** are the ideas or thoughts that pop into your head about doing wrong touching. It might feel embarrassing to talk about these thoughts or feelings, but once you talk about them you can start to control them. Here are three ways to control your impulses:

1. Thought stopping
2. Thought switching
3. Thought (impulse) tracking

Thought stopping is when you have a wrong sexual or angry thought, and you *stop* and think about the consequences.

 ## Assignment 6E

Using a Thought STOP card. Here's how Cedric talks about thought stopping:

> "Sometimes I have thoughts about wrong touching with children. When I have these thoughts I use my Thought STOP cards. These are cards that I carry in my pocket to help me stop unhealthy thoughts that lead to me getting in trouble. When I pull out my card it reminds me that I am in control of my body and that I will get in trouble if I don't control my body."

You and your counselor can decide how these Thought STOP cards will be helpful for you. Here is an example of the front and back Cedric's Thought STOP card:

 I START STARING AT SOME CHILDREN

 I REALIZE I AM FEELING SEXUAL AND THINKING ABOUT WRONG TOUCHING.

 TAKE THREE DEEP BREATHS.

I DON'T WANT TO GET IN TROUBLE.

I CAN CONTROL MY BODY, I CAN TALK TO MY SUPPORT STAFF ABOUT HOW I FEEL, OR I CAN LEAVE THIS SITUATION.

 There is a flash card to remind you to control your thoughts and feelings when you are around people. There are also two blank flash cards with a STOP sign on them for you to make your own Thought STOP cards.

 Assignment 6F

 Thought switching is when you stop the bad thought and change it to thinking about doing something good. This is like changing the channel on the television. You can also use a Thought STOP card to stop thinking about wrong touching and start thinking about right touching or healthy fantasies.

 Thought tracking or **impulse tracking** is when you write down your bad thought so that you don't act on it. Writing down fantasies on your daily diaries is a form of thought tracking. On the next two pages are forms that some people use for thought tracking and fantasy tracking.

 Create a fantasy tracking sheet or make a copy of one that works for you and have it in your scrapbook, use it, and share it with your counselor.

Fantasy Tracking

Name:_____   Date: _____

Use this form to keep track of your sexual fantasies and/or masturbation patterns.

Date	Time	Who was in my fantasy (name and age)	What we did in the fantasy	I masturbated (Yes or No)

Here's another kind of form that you can use to keep track of your sexual fantasies and/or masturbation patterns.

Fantasy Tracking

Name:_____ Date: _____

What unhealthy fantasies did you have?
_____
_____

When were you around kids and what did you do?
_____
_____

What healthy fantasies did you have?
_____
_____

M= _____

What did you think about when you masturbated?
_____
_____

Changing Your Arousal (Also called Arousal Conditioning)

Arousal conditioning is when you decrease your unhealthy (wrong touching) fantasies and increase your healthy (right touching) fantasies. One way to do this is with **covert sensitization**, or CS for short. CS is when you teach your body not to get aroused to fantasies that will get you in trouble. You can do this by using written CS forms or by speaking into a recorder.

 Assignment 6G

Look at Jim's CS form on the next page, which he uses to help him stop his bad fantasies. Then make four copies of the blank CS form on the following page and complete them with your counselor.

Practice CS as often as you can, with your counselor and at home.

 There are four blank flash cards with a STOP sign on them that you can fill out with your counselor to help you get rid of Old Me thinking.

Covert Sensitization

Name: _____Jim_____   Date: ____5-13-2012____

Write out one scene every day for four days, and after writing it, read it back out loud to yourself. Bring this page to our next session.

 Unhealthy (Illegal) Scene — Old Me Thinking:

It is a nice day outside, but I decide to stay inside. I am getting bored. I see some sexy pictures on the television and start to get turned on. I start looking at pictures that I have in my room. I find some pictures of my younger sister and I start looking at them and think about touching her again.

STOP!

 Scary or Upsetting Scene (Like Getting Caught):

Just then my grandmother walks into my bedroom. I am naked with pictures of my sister. My grandmother starts crying. She calls my probation officer and I go to jail.

Positive Choice — New Me Action:

I go outside and exercise and when I feel sexual I go to my room and think about right touching.

Covert Sensitization

Name:_____ Date:_____

Write out one scene every day for four days. After writing it, read it out loud to yourself. Bring this page to your next counseling session.

☠ Unhealthy (Illegal) Scene — Old Me Thinking:

_____
_____
_____
_____
_____

STOP!

🛑 Scary or Upsetting Scene (Like Getting Caught):

_____
_____

Positive Choice — New Me Action:

_____
_____

A similar way to use covert sensitization to help get rid of unhealthy fantasies uses pictures instead of words. You and your counselor can create forms that work for you. First you think about a unhealthy fantasy, then you stop and think about the consequences.

Have fun. Be creative, and STOP your unhealthy fantasies. Here are some pictures that other people used to help them stop having unhealthy fantasies.

Unhealthy (Illegal) Scene — Old Me Thinking:

I get out of the car and go to the store. I see a little girl standing next to the door and I start to think about touching her.

STOP!

 Consequence — What Will Happen:

The girl's father sees me looking at the little girl. He runs over and tackles me. He puts a vise on my head and starts squeezing. I feel like my head is going to pop. I have a huge headache. The man calls the police and they take me back to jail.

 Positive Choice — New Me Action:

Next time I will ignore the girl and look the other way.

Unhealthy (Illegal) Scene — Old Me Thinking:

I am at the beach and I am getting ready to go swimming. I look down the beach and see some kids. I start to think about having sex with them.

STOP!

 Consequence — What Will Happen:

My support staff sees me looking at the kids. Just then a crab grabs on to me and starts pinching me. I scream in pain. The crab won't let go. It hurts really, really bad. Everyone at the beach is staring at me and laughing. I jump into the water.

 Positive Choice — New Me Action:

Next time I won't look at the kids and if I do I'll find another beach.

Unhealthy (Illegal) Scene — Old Me Thinking:

I am going to work. I look out the window and see two kids walking down the street. I start to think about them being naked.

STOP!

 Consequence — What Will Happen:

Just then my seat catches on fire and I start burning. I feel like I am going to die. I try to get out of the car but my thumb gets slammed into the door. I'm screaming in pain.

 Positive Choice — New Me Action:

Next time I'll ignore the kids and talk to my support staff.

 Unhealthy (Illegal) Scene — Old Me Thinking:

I am out shopping and I see a young girl walk by. I start to think about seeing her naked and I can't stop looking at her.

STOP!

 Consequence — What Will Happen:

The girl's father sees me looking at her and he is ready to explode. He comes over to me and punches me. The police get called. I get locked up.

I have to sit and wait while they decide what to do with me. My mother finds out and I feel very bad.

 Positive Choice — New Me Action:

Next time I will get away from the girl and just think about shopping.

Unhealthy (Illegal) Scene — Old Me Thinking:

I am at the beach throwing rocks into the water. I see a small boy playing in the sand. I feel like I can't stop looking at him. He is just wearing shorts and I start to think about touching him. I start to walk towards him.

STOP!

 Consequence — What Will Happen:

Just then his father comes over and starts yelling at me. I get into huge trouble. I get locked up in jail. My stomach starts to hurt as I think about telling my Mom and not being able to go home.

 Positive Choice — New Me Action:

Next time I will tell my support staff person and leave the beach.

3. Express Sexual Feelings in Healthy Ways

Now that we've practiced increasing your healthy fantasies and decreasing your unhealthy fantasies, let's look at how we can express our sexual feelings in healthy ways. Everyone has sexual feelings and it is important to learn what to do with those feelings. First, you must learn to express your sexual feelings in good ways. This means respecting boundaries and remembering what is private and who you can talk to about private things, as we learned in Step 5.

 Assignment 6H

Who can you talk to about private things?

1. _____

2. _____

3. _____

 Assignment 6I

Hygiene (keeping clean) is an important part of being healthy, healthy sexuality, and expressing yourself in good ways. Before you get into a relationship it is a good idea to know how to take care of yourself. Some people put hygiene on their star chart or daily diary. **Hygiene** means keeping your body clean, taking showers, washing your hands, and brushing your teeth, just to name a few important things you should do regularly.

Here is a list of things that people do to help stay clean and looking good:

- Brush teeth
- Floss teeth
- Take a shower every day
- Use soap to wash my body
- Use deodorant
- Wear clean clothes
- Wash hands after using the bathroom and after masturbating
- Wear clean underwear
- Wear clean socks every day
- Wear a belt
- Keep hair combed
- Use shampoo for my hair
- Shave

What are the things that you do to keep your body clean and healthy every day?

1. _____
2. _____
3. _____
4. _____
5. _____
6. _____
7. _____

Boundaries. Okay, now that you look good and are clean, you have to show the people around you that you can respect boundaries . This means you know what is private, just for you, and what is private for other people, just for them and not for you. You learned about this in Step 5. You and your counselor or group can practice this to make sure you know what boundaries are.

When you are in a private place like your bedroom or the bathroom with the door closed it is okay to think about right touching and masturbate. When you get into a relationship with someone it is important to be able to share your feelings in a healthy way. Talk to your counselor about the relationships in your life and what you can do with sexual feelings in your relationships. Feelings should be shared in a way that does not scare or bother people. Another way to express sexual feelings in a healthy way is by being nice to someone you like and showing them that you can respect their boundaries.

Here is how Alan expresses his sexual feelings in healthy ways:

> "I think about my girlfriend and draw a nice picture to give to her. Sometimes when I am alone in my bedroom I think about doing right touching with my girlfriend. Sometimes I ask my girlfriend if I can hold her hand when we watch a movie, but we save the private stuff for a private place like my bedroom."

4. Build Healthy Relationships

By now you are working on having healthy fantasies about right touching, you are decreasing your unhealthy fantasies about wrong touching, and you know how to express your sexual feelings in good ways. Now it is time to learn a little about relationships. The first important part of a relationship is consent. Consent is required for every healthy relationship. You and your counselor and treatment group can make sure that you know how it works.

Here's what Steven learned about consent:

> "Before I knew what consent was, I got into a lot of trouble for wrong touching. Now that I know what consent is, I haven't done any wrong touching for four years and I have a girlfriend. I know that consent means my partner is my age and smart like me, I ask before doing any touching, and we both have the right to say no and be respected, and we know how to protect ourselves from pregnancy and disease. We also know that private part touching is private and should only happen in private places."

You have many different relationships in your life with many different people. Each of these relationships has different boundaries. Knowing the boundaries in your relationships is very important.

Boundaries are important in every relationship, especially romantic relationships. Asking your friend, partner, or girlfriend/boyfriend about their boundaries is very important, and it shows that you care about them. It is also important to talk to them about your boundaries.

 Assignment 6J

Share your boundaries sheet from Step 5 with your counselor or group. Talk to your group about some problems that you have had with boundaries in the past. Then do some role-plays with your counselor or group to practice fixing these problems and respecting boundaries.

Assignment 6K

Now talk to your counselor or group about how you and your girlfriend or boyfriend can talk about your boundaries. Here are some questions to role-play with your counselor or group:

- What touching is okay?
- What touching is not okay?
- How will your partner tell you when you are not respecting boundaries?
- How will you tell your partner when your boundaries aren't being respected?

Another important part of romantic relationships is knowing about sexually transmitted infections (STIs)—also known as sexually transmitted diseases (STDs). Know how to protect you and your partner from STIs and pregnancy. When you are ready, you and your counselor or group can spend time learning more about STIs and birth control.

Assignment 6L

Put your rewards and consequences at the bottom of this chart.

New Me	Old Me
I have healthy fantasies. I can control bad fantasies. I have healthy relationships. I control my sexual feelings and behavior.	Old Me thinking and unhealthy thoughts lead to trouble. The Old Me got in trouble when I did wrong touching. The Old Me didn't think about others.
New Me Rewards	**Old Me Consequences**

Step 6: Sexuality and Relationships
Test

Date: _____

1. If I have a bad sexual thought (unhealthy fantasy) but I change it to a good sexual thought before I do anything, it means that I am going the right way.

    TRUE   or   FALSE

2. Everyone has sexual thoughts.

    TRUE   or   FALSE

3. Having sexual thoughts will get me in trouble.

    TRUE   or   FALSE

4. When is it okay to talk about your sexual feelings?
_____
_____

5. If I like someone and she or he is nice to me then it is okay to do sexual touching with this person.

    TRUE   or   FALSE

6. It is safe to talk to my counselor about my sexual feelings.

    TRUE   or   FALSE

7. It is never okay to masturbate.

    TRUE   or   FALSE

8. It is okay to say sexual things to strangers as long as I don't touch them.

    TRUE   or   FALSE

9. Showing people my private parts is a good way to see if they are interested in me.

    TRUE   or   FALSE

10. It is a good idea to masturbate to bad sexual thoughts to help them go away.

    TRUE   or   FALSE

11. What are three things you can do when you are having strong sexual feelings?

_____

_____

_____

 "I can control my sexual feelings in good ways."

 Your scrapbook should now have the following items from this step:

☐ Healthy fantasy scrapbook

☐ CS forms

☐ Thought STOP cards

 There is a flash card to remind you to have healthy relationships.

Wow! Great work. This was a long step with a lot of information. It will be helpful to come back to this step as you learn more.

STEP 7
Right Thinking

You are in charge of your body and you decide how to control your body. In the past, wrong thinking may have led you to wrong touching and other Old Me behaviors. To stop Old Me behaviors you need to use right thinking. Wrong thinking is what made your wrong touching possible. Now, it is time to learn about right thinking and wrong thinking.

Believe it or not, your brain controls your body. Support staff don't control your body, parents don't control your body, and your friends don't control your body. You control your own body. You control your body with thoughts that come from your brain. If you want to control your body in good ways you have to use right thinking. If you can learn now about right thinking, you will have a much easier time staying out of trouble in the future.

Right thinking is when you tell the truth, when you admit something you did wrong, and when you think about other people, not just yourself.

Here are some more examples of right thinking:

- Thinking of being a good friend
- Deciding to let someone else go first at something
- Deciding to share something nice rather than keep it to yourself

Here are eight words that some treatment groups use to encourage right thinking:

Caring/Sensitivity means thinking about how other people feel and not hurting other people.

Honesty means telling the truth.

Openness means talking about your feelings in good ways.

Respect is when you think about other people, follow rules, and pay attention to boundaries.

Responsibility means taking care of the things that you need to. It also means admitting when you have done something wrong.

Effort means doing your best even when it is difficult.

Courage means being strong even when things are difficult. It takes courage to keep your cool when you are really upset.

Integrity means doing what is right even when it is difficult.

These words can also be called **values**. Having values is part of being a New Me.

✏️ Assignment 7A

What are three values that are important to you? Choose from the list at the left or come up with your own. For example: kindness, working hard, being on time.

1. _____

2. _____

3. _____

⚡ There are eight flash cards to help you to remember these values.

✏️ Assignment 7B

One of the best ways to learn to stay out of trouble is to *always use right thinking*. Give four examples of when you used right thinking during the past week or two. Feel free to ask your support staff, counselor, or family for help with this.

1. I used *right thinking* when I told the truth about:

   _____

2. I used *right thinking* when I showed concern for someone else when:

   _____

3. I used *right thinking* when I helped someone by:

   _____

4. I used *right thinking* when I decided not to:

   _____

Wrong thinking is when you tell a lie. Wrong thinking is also when you only think about yourself. Wrong thinking is when you blame other people for something you have done.

Here are some other examples of wrong thinking:

- Thinking about having sex with a child even if you have never touched the child

- Thinking that people are always picking on you

- Deciding to lie about a wrong behavior so you don't get caught

Thinking Errors

There is another word for wrong thinking. Wrong thinking is also called a **thinking error**.

Thinking errors are bad. Thinking errors make us get into trouble. Thinking errors make it hard to make good choices. In this step we learned that you are in charge of your own body. When you use thinking errors it is hard to control your body. Thinking errors help you not take responsibility for the hurtful things that you do. Taking responsibility is when you

admit the things you've done, the choices you've made, and you agree to the consequences for your actions and choices.

Everybody uses thinking errors every once in a while to avoid getting in trouble or to avoid getting consequences. In *Footprints* you can learn about thinking errors, and you promise to do everything possible to avoid using them in your life.

Following is a list of some thinking errors. There are many more and you can probably come up with some of your own. Maybe you will discover a new type of thinking error. Labeling your thinking errors and creating pictures like the ones on the list that follows can help you pay attention to them and stop using them. You and your counselor or group can act out these thinking errors or set up rewards for catching yourself when you start to use them.

1. **Blaming.** This is finger pointing, or putting the responsibility on someone else. We use this to avoid getting into trouble, or to avoid embarrassment. Sometimes we use blaming to get someone else in trouble.
    Example: "It's not my fault, Tommy made me do it."

2. **Minimizing** or **no big deal.** This is when we make something seem less than it really was. When you hear words like "only" or "just," those are clues that this thinking error is being used. This is when we tell ourselves that what we did was no big deal.
    Example: "I only touched her once." But really it was six times.

3. **Making excuses.** This is when we look only at the "reasons" we didn't do something that we were supposed to do, or when we did something we weren't supposed to. When you hear words like "but," those are clues that someone is making an excuse.

   Example: "But I didn't have time to make my bed because I had to stay up late to finish the movie, so I slept late."

4. **Me, me, me.** When people only think about themselves, this is selfishness. When people want something right away and they don't care about the consequences, we call this *problems with immediate gratification,* or PIG. You feed the PIG when you try to get something without following your rules. You can learn to stop feeding the PIG.

   Example: "I want to play video games so I will skip cleaning up after the dog."

5. **Poor me** or **victim stance.** We use this thinking error to get attention and to make other people feel sorry for us. We also use it to get other people to leave us alone instead of giving us consequences when we mess up. Sometimes we use this thinking error to get others to do things for us that we should be doing ourselves.

   Example: "He called me a name, so I had to hit him and punch a hole in the wall."

6. **Denial.** This is when we pretend that something isn't true when it really is. Sometimes we refuse to face facts

because it makes our lives easier—but only for a while.
Example: "It wasn't me—I was watching TV by myself."

7. **Universals.** These are big global statements about the world that don't leave room for anything else to be true. When you hear words like "always" or "never," those are clues that this thinking error is being used. Any statement that doesn't leave room for anything else is a universal statement.
Example: "The support staff always make me work too hard. They never give me a break."

8. **Assuming.** This is when we act as if we know what is going on, but we don't take the time to make sure. We use this to avoid the responsibility of checking things out with someone else.
Example: "He wanted me to touch him."

9. **Lying.** This involves holding back information and telling only the parts you want to or saying something that is not true. We lie because we don't want consequences.
Example: "I never touched anybody down there!" We can all stop lying if we simply tell the truth, *all the time.*

10. **"I don't know"** or **playing dumb.** This is when we pretend that we don't know the answer. We use this thinking error to avoid telling the truth or to avoid sharing information that we are embarrassed or ashamed about. Most of the time we really know the answer to questions we are asked,

but we don't want to admit it for fear of consequences.

Example: "James, why did you miss group meeting last week?" "I don't know. Was there a meeting? I didn't know about any meeting." To be responsible, we need to stop using "I don't know."

 There are 10 flash cards to help you STOP when you are using thinking errors. There are also four blank cards with a STOP sign so that you can make your own cards for the next assignment.

 ## Assignment 7C

A Thinking Error Card can really help you to remember what is wrong thinking and what is right thinking. Make some cards to remind yourself. Write your wrong thinking or your thinking error at the top of the card, like the ones on the next two pages. Find (or draw) a picture that shows your wrong thinking. Paste it on the card. Underneath the picture write something that will keep you out of trouble when you are doing this wrong thinking. Write the words "right thinking," to remind you of the consequences of wrong thinking. Read your cards every day.

THINKING ERROR
"I'M SLICK"

RIGHT THINKING: BEING SNEAKY AND LYING WILL GET ME INTO TROUBLE.

THINKING ERROR
"I DIDN'T HAVE TIME"

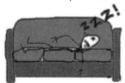

RIGHT THINKING: MAKING EXCUSES WON'T HELP ME GET WHAT I WANT.

THINKING ERROR
"I FORGOT"

RIGHT THINKING: PLAYING DUMB WON'T MAKE THE PROBLEM GO AWAY.

142 Step 7: Right Thinking

THINKING ERROR
"IT WAS NO BIG DEAL"

RIGHT THINKING: MAKING THINGS SMALLER THAN THEY REALLY ARE WILL NOT HELP ME.

THINKING ERROR
"EVERYONE ELSE IS DOING IT"

RIHT THINKING: I WILL NOT LET OTHER PEOPLE GET ME INTO TROUBLE.

THINKING ERROR
"I WANT IT NOW"

RIGHT THINKING: I DON'T HAVE TO HAVE <u>P</u>ROBLEMS WITH <u>I</u>MMEDIATE <u>G</u>RATIFICATION. I WON'T FEED THE <u>PIG</u>.

Use your Thinking Error Cards to stop wrong thinking. Here's how John talks about how he stops wrong thinking:

> "I carry the cards in my pocket and I pull them out when I catch myself using wrong thinking. Sometimes other people on my support team will remind me to use my card if I forget."

 Make copies of your Thinking Error Cards and put them in your scrapbook.

 Assignment 7D

Now for a test! Let's decide if any of the following statements are examples of right thinking or wrong thinking. Your counselor will help you if you miss any. Circle the correct answer:

1. Ricky tells his support staff, "You are right, I did make a mess in my room."

    RIGHT THINKING   or   WRONG THINKING

2. Mary tells her counselor that she did touch her little sister in her private parts.

    RIGHT THINKING   or   WRONG THINKING

3. Richard breaks the TV and explains that it was Dave's fault for calling him a name.

    RIGHT THINKING   or   WRONG THINKING

4. Melissa tells her father, "It is all your fault that I didn't do my chores."

        RIGHT THINKING   or   WRONG THINKING

5. Leroy feels like people are always mean to him, so he thinks it is okay to call them names to get back at them.

        RIGHT THINKING   or   WRONG THINKING

6. Ted wanted his snack right now and started yelling. Later, Ted said, "Well, at least I didn't hit anyone."

        RIGHT THINKING   or   WRONG THINKING

7. A 30-year-old man with touching problems doesn't have many friends. He thinks that he might as well play with the teenagers, since they like him.

        RIGHT THINKING   or   WRONG THINKING

Good work. Your counselor may have more examples for you, and you can probably think of some wrong thinking that has gotten you in trouble in the past.

Assignment 7E

Put your rewards and consequences at the bottom of this chart.

New Me	Old Me
I go the right way when I tell the truth. Right thinking leads me to my goals. I take the right steps when I use right thinking and think about others.	Thinking errors lead to trouble. I get in trouble when I make up excuses. Wrong thinking leads me to consequences.
New Me Rewards	**Old Me Consequences**

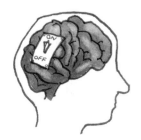

Step 7: Right Thinking
Test

Date: _____

1. When I tell the truth I am using:

      RIGHT THINKING   or   WRONG THINKING

2. When I make excuses I am using:

      RIGHT THINKING   or   WRONG THINKING

3. When I think about the consequences before I do something I am using:

      RIGHT THINKING   or   WRONG THINKING

4. When I hurt someone for being mean to me I am using:

      RIGHT THINKING   or   WRONG THINKING

5. My Thinking Error Card helps me to use thinking errors.

      TRUE   or   FALSE

6. Where do you keep your Thinking Error Cards?

_____

_____

7. When I accept full responsibility for my behavior, I am using:

        RIGHT THINKING   or   WRONG THINKING

8. Blaming someone else for my choices is:

        RIGHT THINKING   or   WRONG THINKING

8. Being honest is wrong thinking.

        TRUE   or   FALSE

9. Name two thinking errors:

_____

_____

 "I will use right thinking."

 Your scrapbook should now include the following item from this step:

☐ Your Thinking Error Cards

 There is a flash card to help remind you to always use right thinking.

Good job. Remember that right thinking leads to rewards and wrong thinking leads to trouble.

STEP 8
Triggers

One way to change your behavior is to look at the things that set you off. We call these triggers. **Triggers** are things that lead you to doing bad things or making poor choices. Triggers might cause you to have strong feelings that you don't know how to control. Sometimes strong feelings can lead to trouble. You will learn more about controlling feelings in a later step. Right now, we want to identify your triggers and find ways to avoid them.

Here's how Noah talks about his triggers:

> "My triggers are: Seeing little girls, seeing little boys, getting yelled at, and looking at nasty pictures. When I see little boys and little girls, I remember my past and I think about having sex with them. When I get yelled at, I feel upset. In the past when I got upset, I made bad choices like fighting. When I see nasty pictures, I start getting turned on to wrong touching."

There are many other triggers. Here is a list of triggers that other people have:

- Being alone with children
- Being bored
- Seeing dirty magazines or pictures of sex
- Getting picked on
- People being bossy
- Not seeing my mom

 Assignment 8A

Now it is your turn to make your own list of triggers. Think of the things that get you upset or lead to you getting into trouble. You can use the ones we just listed, ask your counselor, support staff, or parent for suggestions, or think of your own triggers.

1. _____
2. _____
3. _____
4. _____
5. _____
6. _____

Assignment 8B

Now you know some of your triggers. The next step is to avoid them or make good choices when they happen.

With your counselor, group, or other support person, role-play each one of your triggers. For each one of the role-plays, you can act out a good way to avoid the trigger or a good way to handle the trigger. Once you have acted out all of your triggers, switch roles with your counselor and see some different choices.

One way to avoid triggers is to make a list of them like this one:

My Triggers

Triggers are people, places, feelings, or thoughts that lead to me getting into trouble or hurting other people. My triggers include:

- seeing little girls
- seeing little boys
- getting yelled at
- looking at pornography

I will avoid these triggers.
When I come across triggers, I will get away
from them and make good choices.

Now make a list of your triggers. You can use the blank form below for your list.

 Make a copy of the list of your triggers to share with your support team and have in your scrapbook.

My Triggers

Triggers are people, places, feelings, or thoughts that lead to me getting into trouble or hurting other people. My triggers include:

_____

_____

_____

_____

I will avoid these triggers.
When I come across triggers, I will get away
from them and make good choices.

Now that we know what your triggers are, you will make a plan for avoiding them in the next step. Your plan will help you make different or positive choices to stay away from trouble when your triggers happen. You will learn more about making good choices in the next step.

Assignment 8C

Put your rewards and consequences at the bottom of this chart.

New Me	Old Me
I know what my triggers are. When I handle my triggers in good ways, I get the things I want.	If I forget about my triggers, they will lead to trouble. I get in trouble when I let my triggers control me.
New Me Rewards	**Old Me Consequences**

Step 8: Triggers
Test

Date: _____

1. Triggers are things that help me control my body and stay out of trouble.

   TRUE   or   FALSE

2. If I know my triggers I can try to stay away from them.

   TRUE   or   FALSE

3. If one of my triggers happens I will always get in trouble.

   TRUE   or   FALSE

4. What will you do the next time one of your triggers happens?

   _____

   _____

5. I can practice controlling my behavior before one of my triggers happens.

   TRUE   or   FALSE

6. People who help keep me safe should know what my triggers are.

                TRUE   or   FALSE

7. How can other people help you when one of your triggers happens?

_____

_____

8. What do your triggers look like? Draw pictures of some of your triggers on the bottom of this page or you can cut out pictures to put on this page.

156 Step 8: Triggers

"I know what my triggers are so I can handle them in good ways or avoid them."

Your scrapbook should now include the following item from this step:

☐ Your list of triggers

There are flash cards to remind you that your triggers don't control you.

You are moving right along. Keep up the good work!

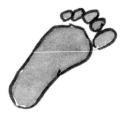

STEP 9
Danger Zones

This step is one of the most important. **Danger zones** are the thoughts, feelings, places, or behaviors that lead to trouble or, even worse, jail. Make sure that you know what they are and how to get away from them and stay away from them. Danger zones are also called **high-risk situations**.

Here are some examples of danger zones:

- Play equipment at the mall, video arcade after school gets out, or grade schools
- Being bored
- Being alone
- Looking at pornography
- Talking to strangers
- Getting yelled at
- Feeling picked on
- Talking to children

Based on your history and your triggers, and using right thinking, you can start to learn what your danger zones are. Remember, danger zones are thoughts, feelings, and places that lead you closer to doing wrong sexual touching and getting in trouble.

One way to find your danger zones is to go back to Step 4 and look at your sexual history. In the last column (life events) there may be some possible danger zones. Another way is to go back to Step 8 and look at your triggers. This is also a good place to find some of your danger zones.

 Assignment 9A

Now it is your turn to make a list of your danger zones.

1. _____

2. _____

3. _____

4. _____

5. _____

Once you have made your list, share it with your counselor to get more ideas. You can also share it with your support team, group, parents, or support staff and ask for their ideas, too.

STOP! This next part is very important. Your list of danger zones can really help you stay out of trouble. Make sure you and your support staff know what they are, so that you will recognize a danger zone when you see one.

GO. Now that you have your list, it is time to label the areas in your life that are danger zones. This is like a treasure map to guide you away from trouble.

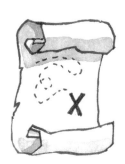

Assignment 9B

1. Draw or take pictures of where you live, where you work, and other places you go.

2. Label the danger zones with a picture or word that works for you.

3. Label the things in the pictures that are private.

4. Draw pictures of danger zones and how to stay away from them.

5. Share your pictures and drawing with your support team so everyone can help you stay healthy.

Assignment 9C

This assignment will help you make a plan for avoiding and escaping danger zones.

 Make a copy of this assignment to share with your support team, have in your *Footprints* scrapbook, or put in a special place.

An **escape plan** gets you out of or away from a danger zone. Here's an example:

> **Danger zone:** There is a video game place in the mall, and I catch my bus near there and sometimes I would like to go play. But that's a danger zone when there are kids there.
>
> **Escape plan:** I ask a staff member to help me find a different bus route that will take me to work. I bring a Game Boy or a Walkman in my pocket so I can play or listen to my music without going into the mall.

First, copy down your list of situations from Assignment 9A. Then make a plan for avoiding and escaping each of these situations.

Danger Zone #1

_____

 Escape Plan #1

_____

_____

 Danger Zone #2

_____

 Escape Plan #2

_____

_____

 Danger Zone #3

_____

 Escape Plan #3

_____

_____

Danger Zone #4

_____

 Escape Plan #4

_____

_____

 Danger Zone #5

_____

 Escape Plan #5

_____

_____

 ## Assignment 9D

Now that you know what is dangerous and you have a plan, you need to practice your plan. You can role play with your counselor, your group, your support staff, and your job coach. Make sure everyone can help you avoid and escape danger zones.

Each time that you meet with your counselor or group you can talk about how you have done avoiding and escaping your danger zones. You may need to add to your list as you get more practice or change your plan as new things come up.

Use this form every day for the next week to show how you avoided a danger zone.

How I Stayed Safe Today

Name:_____ Date:_____

What danger zones did you avoid or escape today?

_____
_____
_____

How did you do it?

_____
_____
_____
_____
_____

Assignment 9E

Put your rewards and consequences at the bottom of this chart.

New Me	Old Me
I know my danger zones. I know how to avoid trouble. I know how to escape trouble.	If I ignore my danger zones, I will get in trouble. If I let myself be in danger zones, I go the wrong way. I go the wrong way when I don't escape.
New Me Rewards	**Old Me Consequences**

Step 9: Danger Zones
Test

Date: _____

1. If Andy has already gotten into trouble for wrong touching with children, then baby-sitting would be a danger zone for Andy.

    TRUE   or   FALSE

2. If Alice has trouble stealing, then going to a store with no money would be a danger zone for Alice.

    TRUE   or   FALSE

3. If Tom was looking at lots of naked pictures during the time he did wrong touching, then looking at naked pictures might be a danger zone for Tom.

    TRUE   or   FALSE

4. I should not tell anyone what my danger zones are because they are embarrassing.

    TRUE   or   FALSE

Step 9: Danger Zones

5. When I meet people at the bus stop it is a good idea to tell them about my danger zones the first time I talk to them.

    TRUE   or   FALSE

6. When I do really well in counseling I can ignore my danger zones.

    TRUE   or   FALSE

7. Who should know your danger zones?

    _____

    _____

8. Who can you talk to about avoiding danger zones? (Circle all that apply.)

    A. My support staff

    B. My boss at work

    C. My Mom

    D. The guy at the coffee shop

    E. My girlfriend

9. How many people have you shared your list of danger zones with?

    1   2   3   4   5   6   more

10. Where will you keep your list of danger zones?

    _____

 "I will avoid my danger zones."

 Your scrapbook should now include the following item from this step:

☐ Your list of danger zones and your escape plans

 There is a flash card to remind you to stay away from danger zones.

Good work. This is a very important step.

Make sure that you share it with everyone

in your support team.

STEP 10
Choices

You learned in Step 7 that you control your body by using your brain. In order to control your body in good ways you need to stay away from triggers, danger zones, wrong touching, and wrong thinking. This step is about using your brain to make good choices. When you use right thinking you are choosing to stay out of trouble.

As you will learn, things don't "just happen." Every time you do something you are making a choice. Because you are in control of your body, your choices decide what happens. In this step you will learn some ways to look at your choices and think before you act.

When triggers happen, sometimes you react. Sometimes you react so fast it feels like you weren't even thinking. Now that you know what your triggers are, you can plan ahead for what to do when they happen. You can even practice making good choices and following your plan by role-playing.

When triggers happen the first step is to *stop* what you are doing and look at your choices or options. By stopping and looking at your choices you can make the best decision, or maybe you will already have practiced making a good decision so it will be easier and take less thinking.

Here's how Ted makes good choices:

> "When one of my triggers happens I have a list of good things that I can do to help me calm down. Once I am calm, I write down my different choices with my support staff. Sometimes I forget to write down my choices and I have to do it after I make a bad choice, but this helps me remember next time."

Every choice you make has consequences. Look carefully at your choices so you can make the best decision. Some choices have good results and some choices have bad consequences.

 Assignment 10A

Make a list of your triggers from Step 8. Then below each trigger list as many choices as you can for how you can react and what you would do.

My Trigger #1

_____

 My Choices

_____

_____

 My Trigger #2

_____

 My Choices

_____

_____

 My Trigger #3

_____

 My Choices

_____

_____

 My Trigger #4

_____

 My Choices

_____

_____

When you go over this page with your counselor or a staff member, explain to them the difference between your good choices and your bad choices. When you know what makes a choice good, you can practice making good choices every day. When you find new triggers and new choices you can add them to your list.

 Assignment 10B

With your counselor, group, or other support person, role-play each one of your triggers from the previous assignment. For each one of the role-plays you will act out your different choices. Once you have come up with as many choices as you can and acted them out, switch roles with your counselor and see some different choices.

Ted talked about writing down his different choices. You can write or think of as many choices as you can. Then once you have your choices, you can use right thinking to make the best choice. This takes a lot of practice.

S.O.D.A.

Here's a way to remember what to do when a trigger happens or when you are in a danger zone: **S.O.D.A.** Not a soft drink, this time. Here's what it means:

S is for **STOP!** Think about your trigger.

O is for **options**, the different choices you could make.

D is for **deciding** what will work best and why you want to do it.

A is for **act**, what you do—or what you did, and what happened after that.

 ### Assignment 10C

Try using the sheet on the next page each time one of your triggers happens. Keep practicing until you can make good choices without the sheet.

 Share this assignment with your support team and put a copy in your scrapbook.

S.O.D.A.

Name:_____ Date:_____

S = STOP when one of your triggers happens. Describe the trigger and the situation:

_____

_____

O = OPTIONS. What are your options or choices?

_____

_____

D = DECIDE. Decide what to do. Explain why.

_____

_____

A = ACT. Do it. What were the consequences?

_____

_____

When you make good choices you get rewards. Making good choices will keep you out of trouble. The more you practice making good choices the easier it will be. When you make mistakes that is a good time to practice making good choices.

Sometimes, even when you make the right choices and use right thinking, you might not get what you want. Maybe the other person will say no. But not getting what you want when you want it doesn't mean that you're bad. Sometimes it means that you have shown respect for someone else to make their own choice. You might be disappointed or even sad, but showing respect and keeping your cool are New Me behaviors that you can be proud of.

Assignment 10D

Put your rewards and consequences at the bottom of this chart.

New Me	Old Me
I go the right way when I think about my choices. I can control what my body does. I can make choices that lead me to good things.	Making bad choices is an Old Me behavior. The Old Me didn't think about what I was doing. Bad choices lead to trouble.
New Me Rewards	**Old Me Consequences**

Step 10: Choices
Test

Date: _____

1. Everybody has choices.

    TRUE   or   FALSE

2. Most choices do not have consequences.

    TRUE   or   FALSE

3. Who controls your body?

_____

4. When I forget that I have choices, I am more likely to get in trouble.

    TRUE   or   FALSE

5. What can you do to remind yourself that you have choices even when you are angry, turned on, or excited?

_____

_____

6. It is easiest to think about my choices when I feel the following: (Circle the best answer.)

   A. Angry

   B. Turned on

   C. Calm

   D. Excited

7. What should someone say when they think that you are about to make a bad choice?

   _____

   _____

"I will make good choices."

Your scrapbook should now include the following items from this step:

☐ Your list of triggers and choices

☐ Your S.O.D.A. worksheet

There is a flash card to remind you to consider your options and make good choices.

Keep making good choices.

You are ready to take the next step.

STEP 11

Feelings

In Step 8 you learned about triggers. **Triggers** are words, places, or things that give you strong feelings. In this step you will learn how to talk about the feelings that are going on in your body in a healthy way. Everybody has feelings every day. Some people are better at talking about feelings than other people. Some people only know how to talk about happy or angry feelings. Other people know about lots of different feelings. To become a New Me it is very important that you learn to talk about lots of different feelings, not just happy or angry feelings.

By learning to talk about feelings, you are learning to get what you want without hurting yourself or other people.

There are many different feelings and many ways to express feelings. You can use words, pictures, noises, art, or make faces, just to name a few ways.

There are three main ways to express feelings. Let's learn these three new words: The first word is **passive** or **cold**. The second word is **aggressive** or **hot**. The third word is **assertive** or **cool**. In this step, we hope that you will learn to be assertive, or cool:

Passive (Cold) means quiet, calm, or idle. Passive people don't react very much. Passive people stay very calm, and nothing bothers them. Passive people don't yell or fight. In fact, passive people sometimes let other people make decisions for them. Shy people are often passive.

Aggressive (Hot) people are pushy, and they sometimes are demanding. They don't always think about how their behavior will affect other people. Aggressive people sometimes scare other people, because they are loud and sometimes mean. Bullies are often aggressive.

Assertive (Cool) people say what they think and they ask for what they want. They are not passive, because they do speak up for themselves, and they do not let other people make decisions for them. Assertive people express their feelings without hurting or scaring other people.

These three words—passive, aggressive, and assertive—describe different ways of expressing feelings. Passive people don't express their feelings enough, while aggressive people express their feelings in a mean or hurtful way. Assertive people express their feelings clearly, without hurting or scaring other people. Being assertive or cool is a New Me behavior.

Let's learn more about how you can be assertive. First, let's look at what makes you happy and angry.

 Assignment 11A

List four things that make you feel happy:

1. _____

2. _____

3. _____

4. _____

 Assignment 11B

Now list four things that make you feel angry:

1. _____

2. _____

3. _____

4. _____

Assignment 11C

Now list four other feelings you sometimes have inside of you (for example: sad, lonely, scared, sexy, frustrated, loving, hungry, tired, cold). If you need more choices, see the list below.

1. _____

2. _____

3. _____

4. _____

Here is a list of other feelings that you might have sometimes. You can act these feelings out with your counselor or treatment group or you can try to use one in your daily diary.

- Anxious
- Confident
- Curious
- Bashful
- Blissful
- Arrogant
- Cautious
- Ecstatic
- Guilty
- Determined
- Interested
- Jealous
- Relieved
- Lonely
- Miserable
- Playful
- Regretful
- Withdrawn
- Sad
- Happy
- Content
- Satisfied
- Sheepish
- Surly
- Hurt
- Exasperated
- Dependent
- Nervous
- Selfish
- Sympathetic
- Bossy
- Sleepy
- Aggressive
- Bored
- Moody
- Loyal
- Shy
- Caring
- Thoughtless
- Tense
- Frustrated
- Angry
- Depressed
- Afraid
- Powerful
- Pleased
- Scared
- Worried
- Hot
- Cold
- Excited
- Silly
- Startled
- Smart
- Irritable
- Shocked
- Loving
- Loved
- Proud
- Thoughtful
- Surprised
- Agitated
- Greedy

Anger

 STOP! This is important. Anger can be an excuse for other feelings!

GO. When you don't want to feel other feelings, like sad or afraid, you might cover up the other feelings by being angry instead. When you use anger to cover up other feelings, you are using a thinking error or wrong thinking. Talking about your other feelings can help you control your anger.

It is okay to get angry as long as you are controlling your body and expressing your feelings in good ways. People who get angry all the time can be described as aggressive. Being aggressive or hot is an Old Me behavior. We have learned that very angry people usually are not very good at talking about their other feelings. So, think of anger as just an excuse to cover up other feelings. There is an example of this on the next page.

Anger Iceberg

Anger is like the tip of an iceberg. All that you see is the tip—anger—and you don't see all the feelings that are hidden under the water. You might get in trouble for acting out your anger, but if you learn to talk about your other feelings the anger will melt away.

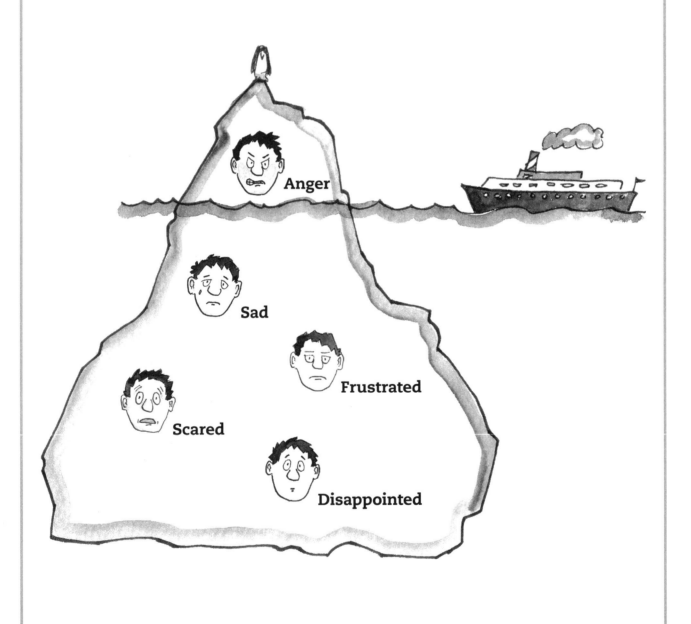

 Assignment 11D

Use the anger assignments on the next two pages to help you make New Me choices when you are feeling angry. The S.O.D.A. assignment from Step 10 can also be used to help you make New Me choices when you are feeling angry. Make copies of these assignments and copies of the S.O.D.A. assignment to fill out for the next two weeks. Use one each time you get angry. (Your counselor can help you make a plan for using the forms.)

 Make a copy of an anger plan or assignment that works for you to share with your support team and put it in your scrapbook. Read it every week. It will only work if you use it.

Controlling your anger is very important. It makes it easier to make friends, keep jobs, and get what you want. It is important to be assertive and manage your feelings in healthy ways.

 There are three flash cards to help you control your anger.

Anger Iceberg

When I get angry I will fill out this anger iceberg about other feelings that I am having like sad, embarrassed, helpless, disappointed, lonely, scared, or bored. I will share this sheet with my support staff or family and talk about my other feelings.

Use this log to help you think about your feelings when you get angry.

Anger Log

Name:_____ Date: _____

Describe what you were most angry about today:

_____

_____

How angry did you get today?   0   1   2   3   4   5

What did you do? _____

_____

Was this a good or a bad way to handle it? Why? _____

_____

If this was a bad way to handle it, what could you do better next time?

_____

_____

How do you think other people felt?_____

_____

What other feelings did you have today? _____

_____

Draw a picture of your anger on a blank piece of paper.

Make a plan for handling your anger in a good way. On the next two pages there are examples that work for other people. You can use these examples or create your own.

When I get angry, I will _____

_____

 Assignment 11E

In the space below, write down as many feeling words as you can. Write down feelings that you have or feelings that you would like to have. It is okay to ask for help from your counselor and to look back at other assignments in this step.

1. _____

2. _____

3. _____

4. _____

5. _____

6. _____

7. _____

8. _____

9. _____

10. _____

 Assignment 11F

Who are the people that you can talk to about your feelings?
List their names:

1. _____

2. _____

3. _____

4. _____

5. _____

 Assignment 11G

Now let's play a matching game. Your job is to match a feeling word with a situation that matches the feeling. Draw a line from each feeling word to the situation that matches the word.

Lonely	Lunchtime
Happy	Bedtime
Frustrated	Doing fun things
Hungry	Not having many friends
Tired	Seeing the bad guys win
Grouchy	Having a family
Sad	Going to the water park
Excited	Getting a hug
Friendly	Getting into trouble
Loving	My cat died
Joyful	Playing with someone i like

Assignment 11H

Think about the last two weeks. Using your own experiences, finish the following sentences:

1. I felt excited when _____
   _____
   _____

2. I felt frustrated when _____
   _____
   _____

3. I felt loved when _____
   _____
   _____

4. I felt happy when _____
   _____
   _____

5. I felt sad when _____

   _____

   _____

6. I felt confused when _____

   _____

   _____

7. I felt lonely when _____

   _____

   _____

8. I felt proud when _____

   _____

   _____

9. I felt afraid when _____

   _____

   _____

Assignment 11I

Sometimes feelings are too strong to make good choices. When this happens it is important to have a plan for how to calm down so that you can deal with your feelings in a good way. Here are some things that Bruce does to calm down. You can use this list or make your own.

THINGS TO HELP ME RELAX

- ASK FOR HELP
- CLAP YOUR HANDS
- TALK ABOUT IT
- LISTEN TO MUSIC
- RELAX
- DRAW A PICTURE
- TAKE THREE DEEP BREATHS

- DO ANGER LOG
- DO A PUZZLE
- TAKE A SHOWER
- TAKE A WALK
- CALL A FRIEND
- DO SOME SIT-UPS

Make your own list of things that you can do to relax or calm down using pictures and words to help make it work. You can use some of Bruce's example and make up some of your own.

1. _____

2. _____

3. _____

4. _____

5. _____

 Make a copy of the things that you can do to relax and share it with your support team, put it in your scrapbook, and use it.

Practice using your list, even when you are not upset. Then when you are ready, you can deal with your feelings in healthy ways and express yourself by being assertive and not hurting other people.

Assignment 11J

Put your rewards and consequences at the bottom of this chart.

New Me	Old Me
I go the right way when I talk about my feelings. I can talk about what makes me angry. I won't let anger control me. I can calm down when I am upset.	The Old Me went the wrong way when I didn't talk about my feelings. The Old Me goes the wrong way when I let anger control my body.
New Me Rewards	**Old Me Consequences**

Step 11: Feelings

Test

Date: _____

1. You go the right way when you are which of the following: (Circle the best answer.)

    A. Passive (cold)

    B. Assertive (cool)

    C. Aggressive (hot)

2. Circle the feelings that you had this week.

    A. Happy

    B. Upset

    C. Lonely

    D. Sad

    E. Another feeling

3. When is the best time to talk about my feelings?

   A. After I get in trouble

   B. When I hurt someone

   C. When nothing is bothering me

   D. Before I act out

4. When is it hard to talk about your feelings?

   _____

   _____

5. Circle the things that help calm you down when you are upset.

   A. Taking a shower

   B. Going for a walk

   C. Punching things

   D. Listening to music

   E. Drawing

   F. Talking to a friend

6. What else helps you calm down?

   _____

   _____

7. Who do you want to control your body when you have really strong feelings?

    A. A police officer

    B. Me

    C. My caseworker

    D. My housemate

"I can express my feelings in good ways."

Your scrapbook should now include the following items from this step:

☐ Your anger plan

☐ Your plan for relaxing

There is a flash card to remind you to express your feelings in good ways.

Well done! Another step completed.

STEP 12
Behavior Cycles

Things that happen in a certain order and repeat are called **cycles**. In a cycle the same steps happen and repeat over and over again. A cycle is like a board game that you go around. Each step in the board game is like a step in the cycle.

 Assignment 12A

Take four sheets of paper. On one of the sheets, write "clap your hands," on one write "blink your eyes," on one write "smile," and on the last one write "nod your head." Place the four pieces of paper on the floor in a square. Now stand on the piece of paper that says "clap your hands" and clap your hands.

Moving clockwise, step on the next piece of paper and do what it says. Repeat this until you are back on the paper that says "clap your hands." This is a behavior cycle.

When you play a board game the dice decides where you go and what you do, but in life you are the boss. With practice, you control where you go and what you do. You decide where to go and what to do. This step can help you learn to make good choices and have good cycles that lead to good things.

People do things in cycles everyday. For example: you wake up, eat, work, sleep, wake up, eat, work, and sleep over and over again. The steps in a cycle can be either positive (good) or negative (bad). Everybody has cycles of behavior.

Once you learn your cycles you can learn ways to stay in a **positive cycle** by making good choices and using right thinking. One type of cycle led to your offending (doing wrong touching). This is called an **offending cycle** and it is especially bad because it can hurt other people and cause bad things to happen to you. This step can help you avoid offending cycles and avoid problem (bad) cycles.

In this step we will learn about your offending cycle that leads to wrong touching and your **negative behavior cycle** that leads to trouble so that hopefully you can learn to have a **positive behavior cycle** that leads to rewards.

Your Offending Cycle

Each time that you did wrong touching you were in your offending cycle and acting out the behaviors or bad steps that led to you offending. Here's how Albert talks about the bad steps that he took:

 It was a normal day and I was feeling good.

 I was looking at naked pictures on the computer.

 I was feeling turned on.

 I was playing alone with my sister.

 I told myself it wouldn't happen again, but I didn't make any plans.

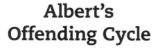
Albert's Offending Cycle

 I used wrong thinking and started to think about touching my sister.

 I told myself it wasn't my fault and it was no big deal.

I started being really nice to my sister and playing alone with her.

 I felt bad for myself and all the trouble that I got in.

 My family found out and I had to go to jail.

 My sister got hurt and she was very scared.

 I touched my sister on her private parts.

These are the steps that Albert went through when he did wrong touching with his sister. Albert worked hard to learn his cycle so that he could change it and make sure that he didn't do those bad things again.

These are the steps that go into every offending cycle. When you did wrong touching all of these steps happened, but they might have happened so quickly you didn't notice. If you have questions or don't understand, ask for help. Now let's think about when you did wrong touching. What were the steps in your cycle?

 Assignment 12B

Remember the last time you did wrong touching, use these pictures and fill in the blanks for your offending cycle.

 Once you complete the assignment on the next page, make a copy of it to share with your support team and put it in your scrapbook.

My Offending Cycle

- How were you feeling before you did wrong touching?
- What trigger happened?
- How did that make you feel?
- What were the danger zones?
- What did you start thinking about?
- What planning or set up did you do?
- What did you do?
- What were the consequences for the victim?
- What were your consequences?
- How did you feel?
- What did you think about what you did?
- Any plans for next time?

Good job. You have now completed your offending cycle. Anything connected to your offending cycle is a danger zone and you need to *stay away*.

Negative Behavior Cycle

Does it ever feel like you keep getting in trouble over and over again, like everything you do, gets you in trouble? This is called a **negative (bad) behavior cycle**.

A negative behavior cycle is any cycle of behavior that leads to you getting in trouble and doing bad things. Negative behavior cycles also use bad thinking for every step. Here is Sean's negative behavior cycle:

Feeling: I WAS FEELING GOOD.	Trigger: MY HOUSEMATE FRANK STARTED YELLING AT ME.	Feeling: I WAS FEELING SAD, UPSET, AND UNSAFE.	Wrong thinking: I THOUGHT OF HOW TO GET EVEN.
Some time passed.	**Sean's Negative Behavior Cycle** 		Bad planning: I GOT THE IDEA OF YELLING AND BREAKING SOMETHING. I DIDN'T THINK I JUST DID.
Planning: I THOUGHT FRANK BETTER NOT DO THAT AGAIN AND I DIDN'T MAKE A PLAN.			Bad action: I YELLED AND BROKE A CHAIR.
Bad thinking: I TOLD MYSELF IT WAS ALL FRANK'S FAULT.	Feeling: I WAS EVEN MORE UPSET.	Consequences for me: I GOT IN TROUBLE AND DIDN'T GET TO GO BOWLING. 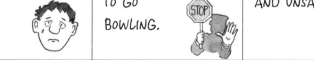	Consequences for them: EVERYONE IN THE HOUSE FELT SCARED AND UNSAFE.

Assignment 12C

Make copies of the blank negative behavior cycle on the next page. Then think of a time in the last couple of weeks when you made a bad choice or did something wrong. Fill in this cycle with your own trigger, feelings, planning, negative behavior, thinking, and consequences. This is your negative behavior cycle. Fill out this form when you make bad choices to make a plan for controlling your behavior in a good way.

 Once you complete the assignment on the next page, make a copy of it to share with your support team and put it in your scrapbook.

Now you know the steps that lead to trouble. As you learned in Step 10, there are always other choices. Each time you take a bad step it makes it harder and harder to get off the cycle. So now you can learn how to change your bad cycles into good cycles that lead to rewards. You will also notice that at the end of the cycle you can think and plan for what to do next. That is another way to use right thinking.

My Negative Behavior Cycle

Feeling?	Trigger?	How did you feel?	What bad thinking did you do?
_____ _____ _____	_____ _____ _____	_____ _____ _____	_____ _____ _____

Some time passes.		What bad planning did you do?
		_____ _____ _____

Any plans for next time?		What did you do?
_____ _____ _____		_____ _____ _____

What did you think about what you did?	How did you feel?	What were your consequences?	What were the consequences for the other person?
_____ _____ _____	_____ _____ _____	_____ _____ _____	_____ _____ _____

Positive Behavior Cycle

Now it is time to learn a new cycle, your positive behavior cycle. This cycle starts out just like your negative cycle with the same steps. You are feeling fine, a trigger happens, and you have bad feelings. STOP! This is where you get to make a choice to move into your positive behavior cycle.

Go back to your negative behavior cycle and look at each step. Think about when you could stop and do something different. Here's how Sean knows when to stop his behavior and look at his choices.

Sean's example:

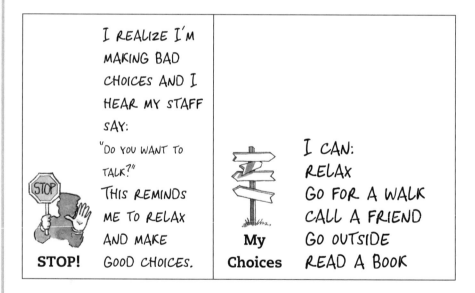

Now let's see how Sean was able to stop his negative behavior cycle and change it to his positive behavior cycle.

Sean's Positive Behavior Cycle

Feeling
I was feeling good.

Trigger
My housemate Frank started yelling at me.

Feeling
I was feeling sad, upset, and unsafe.

I stopped and thought: Frank must really be upset.

Right thinking
I'll leave and go talk to my support staff.

Some time passed.

I stopped and thought: I went over my list of fun things to do.

Planning
Next time, I will be even more ready to stop and make a good choice.

Good planning
I'll invite Frank to go bowling with us.

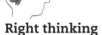
Right thinking
I can control myself and make good choices.

Feeling
I felt great!

Reward for me
I had a great time bowling and didn't let Frank control me.

Reward for them
Everyone had a great time and they saw how well I did.

Good action
We all went bowling.

How do you know when to stop? Pick a bad behavior from your cycle and describe it in the first column; in the second column list your choices.

STOP!	My choices — I can:
_____	_____
_____	_____
_____	_____
_____	_____
_____	_____
_____	_____
_____	_____
_____	_____

Assignment 12E

Now complete your positive behavior cycle, using the form on the next page.

 This is the most important cycle of all. Make a copy of your positive behavior cycle. Once you complete it, share it with your support team and put it in your scrapbook.

If you can remember to use right thinking and express your feelings in good ways, you will get rewarded. Now you can share your behavior cycles with your support team and your group. Your team can help you to choose your positive behavior cycle.

214 Step 12: Behavior Cycles

Feeling?	Trigger?	How did you feel?	How did you stop and think?	What did you think about?

Some time passes.

My Positive Behavior Cycle

How did you stop and think?

Plans for next time?		What planning did you do?

What did you think about what you did?	How did you feel?	What was the reward for you?	What was the reward for others?	What did you do?

Assignment 12F

Put your rewards and consequences at the bottom of this chart.

New Me	Old Me
I go the right way when I use my positive behavior cycle. I can make good choices to get out of my negative cycle. I know how to stay away from the steps in my offending cycle.	The Old Me uses a negative behavior cycle. The Old Me makes bad choices and gets stuck in a negative behavior cycle. The Old Me goes the wrong way when I don't avoid the steps in my offending cycle.
New Me Rewards	**Old Me Consequences**

Step 12: Behavior Cycles
Test

Date: _____

1. Who decides which behavior cycle you are in?

    A. I do

    B. My housemate

    C. My support staff

    D. People who make me mad

2. Triggers can sometimes lead to negative (bad) cycles.

    TRUE   or   FALSE

3. Triggers ALWAYS lead to negative (bad) cycles.

    TRUE   or   FALSE

4. What is one thing that can trigger you into a negative cycle?
_____

5. What will you do the next time that happens?
_____
_____

6. When is the best time to get out of your negative behavior cycle? (Circle the best answer.)

    A. After you get even

    B. When you get in trouble

    C. When the police get called

    D. Early, before you get out of control

7. Thinking about the consequences of my behavior can help me avoid negative cycles.

    TRUE   or   FALSE

8. Thinking errors are part of my positive behavior cycle.

    TRUE   or   FALSE

9. I need to let my negative behavior cycle finish before I can go into my positive behavior cycle.

    TRUE   or   FALSE

10. Write down three things that you can do to get out of your negative cycle.

A. _____

B. _____

C. _____

"I will use right thinking and stop and think so that I can stay in my positive behavior cycle."

Your scrapbook should now include the following items from the step:

☐ Your offending cycle

☐ Your negative behavior cycle

☐ Your positive behavior cycle

There is a flash card to remind you to stay in your positive behavior cycle.

You are moving right along!

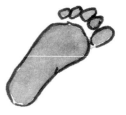

STEP 13
Victims and Empathy

This step is about victims. **Victims** are people who have been abused or hurt or bothered in some way. You may have been a victim of sexual or physical abuse yourself. In this step you will learn about victims in general and the feelings that a victim might have. Next, you will explore your experience as a victim. Finally, you will learn ways of making things better for victims.

Sexual abuse or wrong touching can hurt many different people in many different ways. Victims can include:

- Children who are sexually abused by an older person
- Teenagers or adults who are sexually abused by other people
- People who see someone exposing their private parts to them
- People who receive sexual telephone calls they don't want
- People who have their privacy violated by someone looking at them through a window in their home
- Someone who gets something stolen from them

You and your counselor can probably think of other victims to add to this list.

 Assignment 13A

In the space below, list the people that you have hurt in sexual ways by doing wrong touching. Talk to your counselor and get feedback on your list.

_____

_____

Everyone is different. Everyone reacts to wrong touching or abuse in different ways. Here is a list of some feelings that some victims might have:

- Scared
- Confused
- Angry
- Aroused
- Lonely
- Bored/empty
- Ashamed
- Guilty
- Hurt
- Helpless

If you are a victim of sexual or physical abuse, this is a good time to talk about your feelings. You can also do exercises with your counselor and your group to learn more about these feelings. The next few pages are for people who have been abused. Even if you weren't abused, you should read through these pages. Once you can talk about these feelings in counseling, it may be helpful to tell the person who touched you or hurt you how you felt about it, and what you want from that person.

Sometimes the person who abused you is not in your life any more, but it is still a good idea to try to talk about your feelings. A good way to do this is to put your feelings down on paper in a letter to the person. Sometimes the letter will get sent, sometimes it will not get sent.

For now, try to get your feelings down on paper, and your counselor can help you decide later what you should do with the letter.

What you should put in the letter:

1. Write a greeting, like "Dear Billy."

2. Say how old you are now and where you are living.

3. Say exactly what you remember about the kind of touching the person did to you.

4. Say how you think you felt at that point in time when it was happening.

5. Tell the other person what you want from him or her. For example, "I want you to stop doing wrong touching and get help."

6. Sign the letter with your name.

On the next page there is an example of a letter one young man wrote to his older half-sister who had sexually touched him.

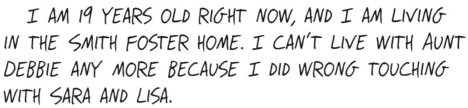

January 1, 2012

Dear Beth,

I am 19 years old right now, and I am living in the Smith Foster Home. I can't live with Aunt Debbie any more because I did wrong touching with Sara and Lisa.

I remember that I learned about touching from you when I was 10 years old or so. You were about 18 years old. I can remember that we were at Dad's old house. I remember that we were in the blueberry patch together, then in the bedroom together. I remember that I had to go to the bathroom. You told me that I could put my penis in your vagina. I remember that it happened two times in one day.

I really don't know how I felt about it back then. Right now I don't feel very good about what you did to me.

I want you to stop touching kids. I think you should go to a counselor to get help. I also want to know why you touched me in the private parts.

Thank you for listening to my feelings. I do care about you since you are my sister.

                                       Your brother,
                                          Ted

Assignment 13B

If you were abused, now it is your turn to write a letter to a person who abused you or hurt you. Your counselor can help you decide who you should write the letter to. Remember, the main purpose of the letter is to help you get your feelings out.

Your counselor will help you decide if you should send the letter or not. If you are in a group, it is a good idea to share the letter with other group members. Sometimes your counselor will even help you meet with the person who touched you so that you can give the person the letter.

Follow the steps we've listed and on the next two pages write a letter to the person who touched you or hurt you.

 Make a copy of this assignment when you are done. Share it with your support team, and put it in your scrapbook.

Date _____

Dear _____,

Sincerely,

Step 13: Victims and Empathy

Good job! Sometimes it can be very hard to think about when you were hurt or when someone did wrong touching to you. Remember to use your calming thoughts about feelings and to talk about your feelings in counseling or with your group or a support team member.

Now it is time to think about the people that you abused or did wrong touching to. Here is what one man in counseling wrote to his sister. He did wrong touching to her when she was little. He wrote the letter with the help of his counselor.

July 1, 2012

Dear Susan,

    I am very sorry I hurt you in the private parts. I am getting help to not do it now. I will not do it again! I can remember touching and hurting you on your private parts about 10 times with my hand. I also touched you and hurt you with my penis. I can understand why you are sometimes scared to be around me. What I did to you was very wrong. I am working in counseling so I will not hurt you again.

    I will not chase you at home, because I don't want you to feel scared. I am also going to follow all of my treatment rules from now on.

                          Your brother,
                           Kenneth

Assignment 13C

Now it is your turn to try writing a letter to the person you touched in a wrong way. Each letter should cover the points listed below:

1. Write down today's date.
2. Greet the person using their name.
3. Say that you want to apologize for your wrong touching.
4. Say exactly what you did to the other person. Describe how you touched the person.
5. Admit it if you lied about it or blamed it on the other person.
6. Say that the touching was your fault (not the victim's fault).
7. Say what you are doing to learn not to do it again.
8. Apologize again for your wrong touching.
9. Promise to not hurt or touch other person again.
10. Sign your name.

Use the next two pages to write your first letter. Don't worry if you mess up! Your counselor can give you more paper to write the final letter.

 Make a copy of this assignment when you are done. Share it with your support team, and put it in your scrapbook.

Step 13: Victims and Empathy

Date _____

Dear _____,

_____

_____

_____

_____

_____

_____

_____

_____

_____

_____

_____

_____

_____

_____

Sincerely,

_____

Nice work! You and your counselor can decide if you should send the letter or not. Sometimes, it is also a good idea to meet with the person to give them the letter and let them ask questions. But in-person meetings only happen if everyone and their counselors agree it is a good thing for everyone. You can also write letters to other victims as well.

 ## Assignment 13D

Put your rewards and consequences at the bottom of this chart.

New Me	Old Me
I can be a good friend.	The Old Me only thought about myself.
I care about how other people feel.	The Old Me doesn't care about others.
When I think about other people I get my goals.	Me, me, me thinking leads to consequences.
New Me Rewards	**Old Me Consequences**

Step 13: Victims and Empathy
Test

Date: _____

1. Empathy means feeling upset when I get in trouble.

    TRUE   or   FALSE

2. Empathy means thinking about how someone else might feel.

    TRUE   or   FALSE

3. Sexual abuse hurts children.

    TRUE   or   FALSE

4. If I write a letter to someone I hurt the person has to forgive me.

    TRUE   or   FALSE

5. People who are sexually abused usually forget about it.

    TRUE   or   FALSE

6. If someone abused me, then it is okay for me to abuse other people.

    TRUE   or   FALSE

7. I always know how other people are feeling.

    TRUE   or   FALSE

8. How can you show people that you care about them?

   _____

9. Circle the items below that show empathy:

   A. Asking friends how they are feeling

   B. Yelling when asked to do chores

   C. Turning down the radio so it won't bother other people

   D. Offering to help someone

   E. Saying you are sorry when you make a bad choice

"I care about myself and I will show that I care about other people's feelings."

Your scrapbook should now include the following items from this step:

☐ Your letter to someone who hurt you

☐ Your letter to someone you hurt

There is a flash card to remind you to think about yourself and other people.

Excellent! You have gotten a lot done.

STEP 14
My Plan for Staying Safe

Most people want to be successful in their lives. In many parts of this country, people with sexual touching problems are given help so that they can learn to stop wrong sexual touching and not have to live in jail. What keeps people out of jail is having a plan for how to stay safe and keep other people safe.

Here's some advice from Richey, a 29-year-old man who has been in counseling for his touching problems for about six months:

> "I have sexual problems, and I have touched young kids in wrong ways. Sometimes it is hard for me to stop. I had a lot of sexual problems, and I almost got put in jail for them. I know one thing for sure—I do not want to go to jail. If you are reading this book, then you probably have the same problem I do. I use my plan to help me stay out of jail and make good choices."

Here are some rules for staying out of jail.

Rules for Staying Out of Jail

1. Never touch someone's private parts if they are not the same age as you.

2. Never touch anybody in any way without asking for and receiving that person's permission first.

3. Do not touch your own private parts except when you are alone in a private place like your bedroom or the bathroom.

4. Don't ever talk to younger children about sex or personal body parts.

5. Don't ever do anything that hurts another person.

6. Don't sneak up on other people.

7. Don't be alone with kids at all, unless another adult is around and watching. This means no babysitting!

8. No wrestling, punching, touching, or grabbing.

9. Do not go into other people's bedrooms for any reason. (This rule may change if you have a relationship with someone your age.)

Assignment 14A

Now make your own list of rules for staying out of jail using words that make sense to you. Go back to your list of rules from Step 1 and add new ones that you have learned.

My Rules for Staying Out of Jail

1. _____
2. _____
3. _____
4. _____
5. _____
6. _____
7. _____
8. _____
9. _____
10. _____

Assignment 14B

You know your rules. This step will help you make a plan for following them. Your Plan for Staying Safe will include your list of rules and your plan for dealing with and avoiding your triggers and danger zones. Triggers and danger zones can be called warning signs that can remind you to use your Plan for Staying Safe. Everyone on your support team should know your plan and make a promise to help you follow your plan.

Begin building your Plan for Staying Safe by listing your triggers and danger zones.

 Triggers (from Step 8)

1. _____
2. _____
3. _____

Danger Zones (from Step 9)

1. _____
2. _____
3. _____

Assignment 14C

You can work very hard to avoid your triggers and avoid your danger zones. But just like everybody else, you will still come into contact with triggers or danger zones at some time or other. It's like being allergic to flowers or bee stings. You can stay away most of the time, but sometimes there are flowers or bees when you don't expect them. When this happens, you need to know what you can do to keep yourself safe. You need to have a plan for what to do and you need to be ready to use your plan.

 For each trigger and danger zone in your list, make a positive plan for how to keep yourself out of trouble. Positive plans use right thinking. Practice using your positive plans to make sure that they work.

My Positive Plan for Trigger #1:_____

_____

My Positive Plan for Trigger #2:_____

_____

My Positive Plan for Trigger #3:_____

_____

My Positive Plan for Danger Zone #1: _____

_____

My Positive Plan for Danger Zone #2: _____

_____

My Positive Plan for Danger Zone #3: _____

_____

 Assignment 14D

Now we will put it all together into your Plan for Staying Safe. This is your plan to keep yourself safe and not do wrong touching again. Your plan keeps you out of trouble if you practice and use it. Here is a blank plan for you to complete, share with your support team, and then use it!

1. Make a copy of your rules for the first page of your plan.

2. Copy the blank plan on the next two pages and fill it out for the rest of your plan.

3. Ask the people on your support team to read the plan and sign the last page.

 Make a copy of this assignment to share with your support team and put in your scrapbook.

My Plan for Staying Safe

This plan is designed to help me stay out of trouble and help me make good choices.

My warning signs	My positive plan
💣	📜
💣	📜
💣	📜
☠	📜
☠	📜
☠	📜

As I find more triggers and danger zones, I will add them to my list and make a positive plan for each one. My support team can also help me by adding to this list.

(continued next page)

My Plan for Staying Safe

This is my plan for staying safe. If you are reading this plan it is because you are part of my support team. I am asking you to help me follow this plan. Let me know if there are things that I should add to it.

_____

I have read this entire plan and I am committed to making this plan work. If I have further input or suggestions I will help add them to this plan. I agree to support this plan fully and will do everything possible to make this plan work.

Name_____ Date _____

Name_____ Date _____

Name_____ Date _____

Name_____ Date _____

Name_____ Date _____

Now you have your plan. It is up to you and your support team to make it work and use it.

 Assignment 14E

Put your rewards and consequences at the bottom of this chart.

New Me	Old Me
I have a plan for going the right way. I can follow my plan for going the right way. When I follow my plan, I get my goals. If my plan doesn't work, I can change it so it will.	The Old Me didn't have a plan. The Old Me got in trouble by not following a plan. The Old Me didn't let people help me follow a path.
New Me Rewards	**Old Me Consequences**

Step 14: My Plan for Staying Safe
Test

Date: _____

1. A plan for staying safe includes warning signs.

   TRUE   or   FALSE

2. How many people can you share your plan for staying safe with? (Circle the best answer.)

   1   2   3   4   5   6   7   8   9   10   More

3. It is a good idea to share your plan for staying safe with your support team.

   TRUE   or   FALSE

4. Where will you keep your plan for staying safe?

   _____

5. Each warning sign in your plan for staying safe should be connected to a positive plan.

   TRUE   or   FALSE

6. What should you do if you stop following your plan for staying safe? (Circle the best answer.)

    A. Go to jail

    B. Give up

    C. Throw it away

    D. Fix your plan to make it work for you, keep trying, and don't give up

7. Whose job is it to make sure you follow your plan for staying safe? (Circle the best answer.)

    A. The police

    B. Your support staff

    C. Your caseworker

    D. Your job

8. What can your support team do if you stop following your plan for staying safe?

_____

_____

9. When you finish *Footprints* you should put yourself in danger zones to show people you don't have a problem.

                TRUE   or   FALSE

10. When you finish *Footprints*, avoiding danger zones should be something that is easy to do.

                TRUE   or   FALSE

 "I will use my plan for staying safe to avoid getting into trouble."

 Your scrapbook should now include the following item from this step:

☐ Your plan for staying safe

 There is a flash card to remind you to use your plan for staying safe.

Good job! A lot of hard work has gone into making it this far.

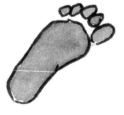

STEP 15
Putting It All Together

By now you have learned about all of the steps that go into living a healthy and happy life. Using all of the steps that you have learned takes a lot of practice and hard work. This is how you get the goals that you want. In this step we will put all of your hard work together so you can remember it, use it, and live it every day.

Many people have learned to be happy using these same steps that you have been learning. We all learn the same steps, but you get to put the steps together into your own walk or journey. You have been creating a scrapbook to help you remember what you have learned and now is a good time to review it. Some people find it helpful to put the information from their scrapbook into a video or a poster to share with their support team.

Your scrapbook is a plan for helping you stay safe. This should be something that you and your support team can use to help you remember all that you have learned.

Here's how TJ talks about his scrapbook:

> "I made my scrapbook two years ago. I keep it safe in my bedroom and I share it with my support team once every couple weeks to make sure it is still working and I am still using what I have learned. Sometimes I forget one or two things, but I just pull out my scrapbook, read it, and then I can remember again."

In this step, we will use the 14 steps that you have learned so far to review everything that has gone into your scrapbook. When you are finished with *Footprints*, your scrapbook will help you make good choices so you can have a happy and successful life. Look at your scrapbook every day to make sure you remember everything. If you forget something that is in your scrapbook look at it again.

Assignment 15A

Reviewing your scrapbook. Your book should include all of the steps described below.

	**Step 1: Who am I?** From this step your scrapbook should include your rules and your self-letter.
	**Step 2: My goals** From this step you should have a list of your problems that you are working on and your goals that you are working toward.
	**Step 3: My promise** You have made a commitment to do right touching and *no wrong touching*. From this step include your commitment to do right touching or rules for right touching.
	**Step 4: My history** You have learned from your history and can share it with others. From this step you should have your sexual history.
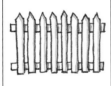	**Step 5: My boundaries** You have learned about boundaries and how to respect them. From this step you should have your boundary sheet.
	**Step 6: My sexual feelings** You can handle and express your sexual feelings in a good way. From this step you should be able to describe how you handle your sexual feelings in good ways.

Step 7: Right thinking
You have learned to use right thinking. From this step, you have made a promise to use right thinking and a list of the thinking errors that you avoid.

Step 8: Triggers
You know your triggers. From this step you have listed your triggers and ways to avoid them.

Step 9: Danger zones
You know how to avoid and escape danger zones. From this step you have a list of your danger zones to avoid.

Step 10: Choices
You know how to make good choices and you have a plan for what you do to make good choices.

Step 11: My feelings
You can express your feelings. These pages describe how you express your feelings without hurting or bothering other people.

Step 12: My cycles
You have made a commitment to use positive behavior cycles.

Step 13: Victims
You know about victims and how to show that you care about other people. From this step you have your letters to victims.

Step 14: My plan for staying safe
You have a plan for staying safe.

Review your scrapbook with your support team and keep it in a special place.

Now you know the difference between right and wrong touching and thinking. You know your triggers and danger zones and how to avoid and escape them. You know your behavior cycles and how to avoid bad cycles. You know about feelings and how to express them.

There is always more to learn. In Step 4 you learned that there were four steps that went into your wrong touching. Now it is time to show that you have corrected those steps so they will not happen again. On the next four pages are assignments that you can complete to help you make steps toward your goals and positive rewards. You can practice making each of these steps lead toward positive (good) behavior. These are good pages to include in your scrapbook.

Way back in Step 4, you learned about the four things that happened before you did wrong touching.

1. You got a bad idea.
2. You used wrong thinking.
3. You did some bad planning.
4. You didn't think about others.

Now it is time to show that you have changed these four things:

1. You want to do good things.
2. You use right thinking.
3. You plan to make good choices.
4. You think about other people.

You are a New Me.

 Assignment 15B

On the next four pages you can fill in each page with good choices. What good things do you want to do? What do you think about to help you stay safe? What are the things around you that help you stay safe? How do you treat the people around you?

 Make a copy of this assignment to share with your support team and to put in your scrapbook.

Motivation or Idea

Here are some good things that I like to do and look forward to doing:

_____

_____

_____

_____

_____

_____

_____

_____

_____

_____

_____

_____

_____

Decide If It Is a Good Idea or a Bad Idea

These are the things I think about to help me stay safe and make good choices:

_____

_____

_____

_____

_____

_____

_____

_____

_____

_____

_____

_____

_____

_____

My Planning

Who and what things help me stay safe:

___
___
___
___
___
___
___
___
___
___
___
___
___
___

Other People

How I like to treat other people:

One of the most important parts of this assignment is sharing it with your support team and using all that you have learned. *Remember, we never stop learning.*

 Assignment 15C

Put your rewards and consequences at the bottom of this chart.

New Me	Old Me
I know the steps to staying safe. I will take the steps to stay safe. I will never stop learning and growing and I will get my goals.	The Old Me doesn't learn from mistakes. The Old Me forgets what I have learned. Being lazy and forgetting what I have learned is an Old Me behavior.
New Me Rewards	**Old Me Consequences**

Step 15: Putting It All Together
Test

Date: _____

1. How will you remember all of the good things that you have learned in this book? (Circle the answers that work for you.)

    A. Practice what I have learned

    B. Share what I know with other people

    C. Throw away my book so that I never do bad things again

    D. Talk to people on my support team

    E. Hang out in dangerous places now that I am safe

    F. Don't give up even when I make mistakes

2. Who will you share your scrapbook with? (Circle all that apply.)

    A. My family

    B. My close friends

    C. My support team

    D. My probation officer

3. Where will you keep your scrapbook?

   _____

   _____

4. What will you do if you stop following your safety plan? (Circle the best answer or write in your own answer.)

   A. Talk to my counselor and make a plan for getting back on track

   B. Review my safety plan with someone on my support team

   C. Work on adding information to my scrapbook

   D. _____

5. The only way my scrapbook will work is if I use it.

   TRUE   or   FALSE

6. What can people say or do to help you remember to use what you have learned?

   _____

   _____

7. What is the most important thing that you have learned in treatment?

   _____

"I will practice taking healthy steps everyday."

Your scrapbook should now include the following from this step:

☐ Everything that you have learned put together so you can share it and use it

There is a flash card reminding you to practice taking healthy steps every day.

Nice work! Now you are ready for the last step.

STEP 16
Living the Steps

Now you have put it all together. The next step is keeping it all together and continuing to live the steps that you have learned. Remember you can always go back and review steps as you learn more. You wrote a self-letter in Step 1. In this step, you will write a new self-letter that includes all of your progress. Before you start your new self-letter, go back to Step 1 and read your old self-letter.

 Assignment 16A

Answer the questions on the next few pages to write a new self-letter.

 Make a copy of this assignment to share with your support team and put it in your scrapbook.

Step 16: Living the Steps

Date _____

Dear _____,
      (You)

1. Who are you (how old are you, where do you live)?

   _____
   _____
   _____
   _____

2. Describe how you feel about yourself now. Include five positive things that you like about yourself.

   _____
   _____
   _____
   _____
   _____
   _____
   _____

3. How do you feel about what you have learned in *Footprints*?

_____
_____
_____
_____
_____

4. What do you think would lead you to bad touching again?

_____
_____
_____
_____
_____

5. What things are you still working on?

_____
_____
_____
_____

6. What are the good activities and interests that keep you going the right way?

   _____
   _____
   _____
   _____
   _____

7. What are your goals for 6 months from now?

   _____
   _____

   1 year from now? _____
   _____
   _____

   5 years from now? _____
   _____
   _____

8. How will you get to your goals?

_____
_____
_____
_____
_____
_____

9. What are the main things you have learned in treatment?

_____
_____
_____
_____
_____
_____
_____

Sincerely, _____
(You)

266 Step 16: Living the Steps

 Assignment 16B

On the next few pages there are some questions that you can answer to show yourself and your team all of the progress that you have made. This will be a contract that you will follow to help you make healthy steps and stay out of trouble.

Healthy Living for a New Me

Name: _____ Date: _____

Date you started treatment: _____

Your age now: _____

1. What is your long-term plan for being around children?

   _____

   _____

   _____

2. How will you handle drugs and alcohol in your life?

   _____

   _____

   _____

3. In the future, who will you have to tell (disclose) your history to?

_____

_____

4. What relationships do you plan on having in the future?

_____

_____

_____

5. What is your plan for work?

_____

_____

6. What is your plan for staying safe?

_____

_____

7. What positive and healthy activities do you plan to have in your life?

___

___

___

___

___

When you complete this assignment, make a copy and share it with your support team, then put a copy into your scrapbook.

Assignment 16C

Now is a good time to review your list of rules. Your rules may have changed as you made progress in treatment. Everybody has rules that they follow. What are your rules that you will keep following?

 Share your rules with your support team and put a copy into your scrapbook.

My Rules

1. _____
   _____

2. _____
   _____

3. _____
   _____

4. _____
   _____

5. _____
   _____

Assignment 16D

My support team. These are all the people that help you follow your rules so that you can get what you want in good ways. Your support team is an important part of every step that you have made and will continue to be an important part of your life.

Write the name of each person on your support team:

_____

_____

_____

_____

_____

_____

Your support team may change as you make progress and you will need to keep your team onboard with what you are working toward and how they can help. It is your job to live the steps, use your support team, and continue the path. Keep working on your goals. Your counselor may have other resources for you to work on as you continue to make progress.

Assignment 16E

Fill in your rewards at the bottom of this chart.

New Me
In the space below, draw pictures, write, or paste pictures of all the good things you get when you take the right steps.
New Me Rewards

Step 16: Living the Steps
Test

Date: _____

1. Everyone has rules that they can follow.

                   TRUE   or   FALSE

2. Sometimes other people decide whether or not I follow my rules.

                   TRUE   or   FALSE

3. What are two of the rules that you will always follow?
   _____

4. What is the biggest thing that you will have to watch out for to keep safe?

   A. Controlling my anger

   B. Not getting aroused by children

   C. Not stealing

   D. Respecting boundaries

   E. Write in another: _____

5. Now that I am done with *Footprints* there are no other goals that I am still working on.

TRUE   or   FALSE

6. I know my rules and I can follow them.

TRUE   or   FALSE

7. I can control my anger and treat other people with respect.

TRUE   or   FALSE

8. I will always be learning new things and setting goals for myself.

TRUE   or   FALSE

9. What was the hardest thing to learn in counseling?

_____

_____

10. I will not give up when I make mistakes.

TRUE   or   FALSE

Step 16: Living the Steps

"I will never stop learning to take healthy steps."

Your scrapbook should now include the following items from this step:

☐ Your new self letter

☐ Your Healthy Living for a New Me contract

☐ Your rules

There is one last flash card.

Great job! You have taken all the steps in *Footprints*. You have done a lot of work and you can be proud of yourself. If you are a good reader, you may want to ask your counselor for other treatment work. If you forget some of the steps that you have learned in this workbook, it is your support team's job to get you back on track, review the information, and help you keep practicing it. For now, feel proud that you did all the work in *Footprints*.

Congratulations!

You have made it to the end of *Footprints*. If you are like other people who have finished this book, you have goals that you are still working toward. It might be a good idea to share your new safety plan book with someone on your support team.

We are always growing and always learning. As you learn more, it is important to set new goals, find new ways to grow, and keep taking healthy steps.

Words to Know

aggressive (hot) — expressing your feelings in a way that hurts or bothers other people—**hot**

assertive (cool) — you say what you feel and you ask for what you want without hurting other people—**cool**

caring/sensitivity — thinking about how other people feel and not hurting other people

consent — when someone agrees to do something, they understand, and they are your age

consequences — trouble for doing something wrong or bad

communication — talking about your feelings

courage — being strong and keeping your cool even when things are difficult

danger zones — people, places, or thoughts that lead to you getting into trouble; same as **high-risk situations**

effort	doing your best even when it's difficult
empathy	thinking about other people's feelings
fantasies	thinking about sex or sexual touching
healthy fantasies	thinking about good touching that won't get you in trouble or hurt other people
high-risk situations	people, places, or thoughts that lead to you getting into trouble; the same as **danger zones**
honesty	telling the truth
hygiene	the things you do to keep your body clean
integrity	doing what is right even when it is difficult
masturbation	touching your private parts to make yourself feel good
openness	talking about your feelings in a good way
passive (cold)	quiet, calm, or idle; passive people don't react very much and they don't talk about their feelings—**cold**
private	just for you or just for him or her
public	for everyone

respect	thinking about other people and following rules and boundaries show that respect other people
responsibility	taking care of the things you need to and admitting when you have done something wrong
rewards	these are the things and feelings that you get or want when you go the right way
right thinking	thinking about the consequences and telling the truth
right path	doing things that keep you safe and don't hurt or bother other people
self-talk	these are the things that you say to yourself to stay safe
STOP!	this picture comes before things that are extra important in this book
support team	these are the people in your life who help you
thinking errors	these are the bad thoughts or wrong thinking that lead to you to trouble

triggers these are things that give you strong feelings

unhealthy fantasies thinking about wrong touching or touching that would get you in trouble

victims anyone who is hurt or bothered is a victim

wrong path doing things that hurt you, hurt other people, and lead to trouble